NAVIGATING

A GUIDE TO FAITHFULLY READING

GOSPEL

THE ACCOUNTS OF JESUS'S LIFE

TRUTH

REBECCA McLAUGHLIN

Lifeway Press®
Brentwood, Tennessee

Published by Lifeway Press® • © 2023 Rebecca McLaughlin
No part of this book may be reproduced or transmitted in any form or by any means, electronic or mechanical, including photocopying and recording, or by any information storage or retrieval system, except as may be expressly permitted in writing by the publisher. Requests for permission should be addressed in writing to Lifeway Women Bible Studies, Lifeway Resources, 200 Powell Place, Suite 100, Brentwood, TN, 37027-7707.

ISBN: 978-1-0877-6837-3 • Item: 005838277
Dewey decimal classification: 232.9
Subject headings: JESUS CHRIST \ BIBLE. N.T. GOSPELS \ BIBLE. N.T.—HISTORY OF BIBLICAL EVENTS

To order additional copies of this resource, write to Lifeway Resources Customer Service; 200 Powell Place, Suite 100, Brentwood, TN, 37027-7707; order online at lifeway.com; fax 615.251.5933; phone toll free 800.458.2772; or email orderentry@lifeway.com.

Printed in the United States of America

Lifeway Resources
200 Powell Place, Suite 100,
Brentwood, TN, 37027-7707

Cover design by Christi Kearney

EDITORIAL TEAM, LIFEWAY WOMEN BIBLE STUDIES

Becky Loyd
Director, Lifeway Women

Tina Boesch
Manager

Chelsea Waack
Production Leader

Mike Wakefield
Content Editor

Erin Franklin
Production Editor

Lauren Ervin
Art Director

Sarah Hobbs
Graphic Designer

TABLE OF CONTENTS

HOW TO USE THIS STUDY

Welcome to *Navigating Gospel Truth: A Guide to Faithfully Reading the Accounts of Jesus's Life.* This study will expand your understanding and application of Scripture as you explore the different literary genres and devices used by the Gospel writers to communicate the life and teachings of Jesus.

Because we believe discipleship happens best in community, we encourage you to do this study together in a group setting. Or, if you're doing this alone, consider enlisting a friend or two to go through it at the same time. This will give you study friends to pray with and connect with over coffee or through text or email so you can chat about what you're learning.

HOW TO WATCH YOUR VIDEOS

With the purchase of this book, you have access to teaching videos that provide content to help you better understand and apply what you just studied in the previous session. **You'll find detailed information for how to access the teaching videos on the card inserted in the back of your Bible study book.**

WHAT'S INSIDE

HERE ARE SOME THINGS YOU'RE GOING TO FIND IN THE STUDY:

Group Pages: As you meet with your group each week, these pages provide a place to take notes from the video teaching and discussion questions to debrief the video teaching.

Personal Study: Each week you'll have five days of personal study.

Tips/Exercise: At the conclusion of Sessions Two through Seven, you'll find closing pages that include important highlights of the specific genre or device studied in that session, plus an exercise to help you apply what you've learned.

LEADING A GROUP?

Whether a large or small group, we have what you need to lead women through *Navigating Gospel Truth*. Visit **lifeway.com/gospeltruth** for free leader downloads, including a Leader Guide PDF, promotional resources, and more.

ABOUT THE AUTHOR

Rebecca McLaughlin holds a Ph.D. in Renaissance Literature from Cambridge University and a theology degree from Oak Hill College in London. She is the author of *Confronting Christianity: 12 Hard Questions for the World's Largest Religion* (2019), which was named book of the year by *Christianity Today*, and of *10 Questions Every Teen Should Ask (and Answer) about Christianity* (2021), *The Secular Creed: Engaging 5 Contemporary Claims* (2021), *Is Christmas Unbelievable? Four Questions Everyone Should Ask About the World's Most Famous Story* (2021), and *Confronting Jesus: 9 Encounters with the Hero of the Gospels* (2022). She lives in Cambridge, Massachusetts, with her husband, Bryan, her two daughters, Miranda and Eliza, and her son, Luke.

INTRODUCTION

"Would you leave your mummy if she needed you?"

I was near the top of the ski slope and my nine-year-old Eliza was looking at me intently. Over the last few years, my husband, Bryan, (who can ski backward, forward, sideways, and probably upside down for all I know) has been teaching our girls to ski while I took care of their baby brother. But this year, Luke turned three and was deemed old enough to learn. Bryan undertook his training, while Miranda (eleven) and Eliza (nine) helped me. I've only skied for three days in my life, and I've spread those days over three decades, so I'm truly terrible. But Eliza was especially patient with me, despite clearly wishing she could go off and have fun with her sister. I told her she should go. She said no. I said, "Really, I'll be OK." She said, "No, it's fine." I said, "I want you to have fun!" That's when she asked if I'd abandon my own mother if she needed me, and I shut up. Secretly, I was thankful she hadn't left.

In one sense, skiing is straightforward. You get lifted up a mountain with long, slippery things on your feet. Then you slide back to the bottom again. But it's not actually that simple. If you just stand on the mountain and point down, you'll soon find yourself in a painful and humiliating heap. (Trust me—I've been there!) You need to practice balancing on your skis, controlling your speed, and navigating the terrain. There are parts of the run where you can just go straight down and take in the view. But much of the time you need to zigzag back and forth, and sometimes bumps and jumps and icy patches can throw you off. A three-year-old can get the hang of it. But it takes work.

When it comes to reading the Gospel accounts of Jesus's life, we're faced with an exhilarating ride and an utterly breathtaking view. But to navigate the Gospels well, we need to get a sense of what the Gospels are, we need to find our feet, and we need to get a grasp of the terrain. This Bible study is designed to help you do just that. We'll look together at the different kinds of writing that we find in the four Gospels, and we'll get some practice on the slopes.

In Session One, we'll ask why we should trust the Gospels as authentic biographies of Jesus in the first place. We'll get a sense of when they were written and by whom, and why we should believe they give us access to the actual life and teachings of Jesus of Nazareth.

Session Two will look at narrative: how the Gospel authors tell us stories about Jesus and what we should make of the differences between the ways that different Gospel authors tell us the same story.

In Session Three, we'll explore metaphor and see that some of the most important and demanding truths the Gospel authors tell us are packaged in non-literal language.

Session Four will focus on the stories Jesus told and how His parables sift His audience: pulling those who have ears to hear in and pushing those who don't really want to hear from Jesus out.

In Session Five, we'll look at five other teaching tools that Jesus used: hyperbole, commandment, blessing, contradiction, and aphorism. Like moguls on the ski slope, these can throw us off if we're not aware of how they work.

Session Six will work through five examples of dialogue in the Gospels. We'll see Jesus laying down challenges to His conversation partners and note how His listeners respond to the push and pull.

In Session Seven, we'll tackle prophecy from different angles, discovering how understanding more of prediction, poetry, personification, and apocalyptic can help us navigate prophecy in the Gospels.

Finally, in Session Eight, we'll reflect on what we've learned and chart the course ahead from here!

On my most recent ski day, I only attempted one green run. I did it a couple of times, and I began to get a sense of the mountain from that slope. At points, it intersected with another run, and I had to be careful to steer toward the "family slope" when the runs diverged again. If I'd grown my skills enough, I could have tried skiing other slopes and gotten to know the mountain more. But one run was all I could handle that day! The Gospels of Matthew, Mark, Luke, and John offer us four distinct-but-connected paths through Jesus's life. They all arrive in the same place, and at times, two Gospels fully intersect. But to read each Gospel well, we need to get a sense of how the four biographies of Jesus complement each other—even when, at first glance, they might look like they contradict.

I'm terrified much of the time when I'm trying to ski, and there might be times in the coming weeks when the terrain feels scary or disorienting. But as we get better at reading the Gospel accounts, my hope is we'll all become more captivated by the view of Jesus they offer, more confident in our understanding of the Gospel story, and more certain that Jesus really is the Son of God, who came to give His life for us so we could live with Him forevermore.

Just as practicing on one slope helps you when you're faced with others, I hope this time spent in the Gospels will equip you to read other parts of the Bible more faithfully too. Each book in our Bibles is built on the mountain of Christ. So, it's worth tackling the double black diamonds! But in this study, we'll stay on the Gospel slopes and see how different kinds of writing help us understand who Jesus is.

Perhaps when you've finished the course, you can think of someone in your life who might be ready to go through it with you, similar to how Eliza was ready to coach me on the slopes. Like mine, that person's progress might be slow at first. But we all learn faster when we stick together, and sometimes teaching someone else is the best way to really cement what you've learned for yourself.

Let's get started!

Rebecca McLaughlin

WHY TRUST

the Gospels?

When people ask me why I am a Christian, I sometimes answer: "*The Lord of the Rings.*" It's not the whole story, but my dad read me J. R. R. Tolkien's unbelievable books when I was a kid, and entering his beautiful, fictional world made me yearn for an even more beautiful reality. The authors of the Gospels welcome us into that much more beautiful world: it's our world seen through different eyes, with Jesus at the center of it all.

It's not that the Gospels paint a shiny, happy, sugarcoated picture of reality. Just like in Tolkien's fictional world, painful, terrible, and heartbreaking things happen in the real world of the Gospels again and again. But Jesus walks right through the heartbreak— even death itself—and comes out on the other side. The authors of the Gospels offer us the opportunity to follow Jesus into what Matthew, Mark, and Luke most often call "the kingdom of heaven" or "the kingdom of God," and John's Gospel tends to call "eternal life"—a world where Jesus is the King and all that's wrong will be put gloriously right.[1] But in order to take their offer seriously, we need to ask ourselves if we can trust these Gospel authors. Are they writing four biographies of one first-century, Jewish man known as Jesus of Nazareth, who lived in history and died upon a Roman cross? Or are they more like Tolkien: creating a beautiful, fictional world?

This week, we're going to ask some searching questions, like, "Who wrote the Gospels anyway?"; "Weren't they written too long after Jesus's life to be trusted?"; "Don't they contradict each other?"; and "How do we know we even have the right Gospel texts and that their message hasn't been lost in translation?"

Instead of being unreliable mythologies, as some skeptics suggest, we'll see that all four Gospels were written well within the lifetimes of the eyewitnesses to Jesus's life and that they record authentic testimony about historical events. We'll think about translation and how we can be confident we're getting access to what Jesus really did and taught. We'll also take a snapshot of the process used by scholars to determine that the texts in our Bibles reflect the texts the Gospel authors wrote so many centuries ago.

In our study this week, we'll only be able to scratch the surface of the questions you might have. To learn more, I recommend two recent books: *Can We Trust the Gospels?* (2018) by New Testament scholar Peter J. Williams and *Why I Trust the Bible* (2021) by William D. Mounce. The more I've looked into these questions for myself, the more confident I've felt that the Gospels are reliable biographies of Jesus. My hope is that after this first week of study you will feel the same.

SESSION *One*

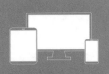

To access the video teaching sessions, use the instructions in the back of your Bible study book.

NOTES

Watch Rebecca's Session One video.

1. The Gospels are early
- Mark was written first
- diciples traveled everywhere w/ Jesus
- John is last gospel written

2. Gospels are eyewitnessed
- Gospel accounts specific eyewitnesses
- Sussanah, Mary, & Joanna
- Mark 10:46-52 - Bartameus

3. Gospels are edits
- many similarities & many differences
- edit them to help us focus on specific things

4. Gospels are embarressing
- argues against idea that Gospels were written for political agenda
- Mark 14:26-31
- Mark based on peter's memory
- women were considered unreliable, but they are eyewitness listed in gospels

5. Gospels are everywhere
- we dont have originally manuscrpts, but these Gospels spreaded so early & we can compare copies across countries

Download the *Navigating Gospel Truth* leader guide at **lifeway.com/gospeltruth**

GROUP DISCUSSION GUIDE

Which of the evidences for why we should trust the Gospels is most compelling to you? Why?

- Gospels are edits. confinms that they are the same stories & the differing details were intentional to highlight specific things

What is significant about women being named in the Gospels?

- women were considered unreliable witnesses so they wouldnt have been included if it didnt actually happen. Embarresing for writers

How does the inclusion of embarrassing moments for some characters increase the Gospels' credibility?

Proves that writers werent just doing it to make themselves look good. If they wanted to do that, certain things wouldnt have been included

Do you feel better equipped to answer someone's doubts about the authenticity of the Gospels? Explain.

Yes & No. I think I just still need more info. I think actually reading Gospels will help w/ that

What part of the video teaching was most important for you?

Gospels are everywhere

THE AUTHORS

When people ask me what my favorite work of fiction is, I'm torn between the aforementioned *The Lord of the Rings* and Jane Austen's *Persuasion*. Both Tolkien and Austen were deeply influenced by their Christian faith. Far from being just a cultural Christian, Austen wrote family devotions for her and her sister, including prayers where she asked the Lord to protect them from missing out on salvation and being "Christians only in name."

Since her death, Jane Austen has become extremely famous. But during her lifetime, her novels were published anonymously. Her first book, *Sense and Sensibility*, simply declared that it was written "By A Lady." Her second, *Pride and Prejudice*, was "By the Author of *Sense and Sensibility*." Her third, *Mansfield Park*, was "By the Author of *Sense and Sensibility* and *Pride and Prejudice*." You might be spotting a theme! When it comes to novels, what matters is the quality of the writing, not who wrote it. We might be very interested to know the author once we've fallen in love with the book. But the book stands on its own two fictional feet.

Biographies are different. If I'm reading a biography, I want to know the author isn't writing fiction. I want to know the author has done his or her research. The identity of the biographer doesn't matter in and of itself. But I need to know the author is a reliable guide to the person he or she is describing, not just someone who is good at making things up. So, what do we know about the authors of the four biographies of Jesus known as Matthew, Mark, Luke, and John?

None of the Gospels names its author, and only one of them claims directly that its author was an eyewitness of Jesus's life. A bit like Jane Austen when she called herself "the Author of *Sense and Sensibility*," the author of John's Gospel called himself "the disciple Jesus loved." But the names Matthew, Mark, Luke, and John were attached to the four Gospels very early on—very likely as soon as they were being passed around the first- and second-century churches—and we get clues about who those authors were both in our Bibles and in other early Christian writings. Today, we're going to track down some of those clues.

MARK'S GOSPEL

Most experts agree that Mark's Gospel was written first. Even non-Christian scholars date Mark between thirty-five and forty-five years after Jesus's death (i.e., between AD 60 and 70). Some Christian scholars think it was written even earlier. Either way, Mark was written well within the lifetime of eyewitnesses to Jesus. So, who was Mark, and how do we know he was consulting with these witnesses? A Christian leader named Papias, who was writing around the turn of the first century (roughly AD 95–110), recorded the testimony of a man known as John the Elder, who said that Mark based his Gospel on the memories of the apostle Peter, who was one of Jesus's closest friends.

This testimony lines up with what we learn about a man named Mark in Acts 12. That chapter tells how Peter was led out of prison by an angel in the middle of the night. At first, he thought he might be dreaming but then realized he was out of the prison and went to find the other Christians.

READ ACTS 12:11-14. What things do we learn about a man named Mark in verse 12?

How does this story add weight to Papias's claim that Mark wrote his Gospel based on Peter's memories?

We also find a reference to Mark in Peter's first New Testament letter.

READ 1 PETER 5:13. How did Peter describe Mark?

This doesn't mean that Mark was literally Peter's son. But it does mean that Peter was Mark's mentor. So, Mark had lots of opportunities to consult with Peter and other eyewitnesses of Jesus's life. In Acts 12:25, Colossians 4:10, and Philemon 24, we find that Mark was also a close companion of the apostle Paul. Paul did not know Jesus during His earthly ministry, but he was well known to the other apostles and was given specific revelation from God.

How does Mark's relationships with two apostles (Peter and Paul) give us confidence in him as a biographer of Jesus?

MATTHEW'S GOSPEL

Matthew's Gospel is generally agreed to be later than Mark's, with many experts dating it between AD 60 to 80. Papias also mentioned Matthew, suggesting that he may originally have written his Gospel in Hebrew or Aramaic (the common language of Jews of Jesus's time and place). Matthew, Mark, and Luke all include someone named Matthew in their lists of Jesus's twelve apostles (Matt. 10:3; Mark 3:18; Luke 6:15).

READ MATTHEW 10:2-4. What do we learn about Matthew from these verses?

Like Simon, whose other name was Peter, it seems that Matthew also had another name.

READ MATTHEW 9:9, MARK 2:14, AND LUKE 5:27. What was Matthew's other name?

The apostle Matthew didn't play a big role in any of the Gospels, but our earliest evidence suggests that this Matthew became a biographer of Jesus and wrote the Gospel known by his name.

LUKE'S GOSPEL

Luke's Gospel was likely written at a similar time to Matthew, between AD 60 and 80. But unlike the other Gospel authors, Luke went on to write a sequel, which we know as the book of Acts. Luke was also a companion of Paul's.

READ COLOSSIANS 4:14. What do we learn about Luke from Paul's description?

READ 2 TIMOTHY 4:11. What do we learn about Luke and Mark from these verses?

This verse indicates that both Mark and Luke were part of Paul's inner circle of ministry partners, meaning they probably would have known each other.

Mark is the shortest Gospel. It takes about an hour and a half to read. Luke is the longest and takes about two and a half hours to read. How does the difference in length help us understand why Luke might have wanted to write a Gospel, even if he was already aware of Mark's and had read it?

JOHN'S GOSPEL

Most scholars think that John's Gospel was the last one to be written, around sixty years after the events it records (approximately AD 90–95). But it's also the only Gospel that claims in the text itself to have been written by an eyewitness. The name John was attached to this Gospel from the earliest records we have, and by the end of the second century, its author was being identified with John the son of Zebedee, who was one of Jesus's twelve apostles. Many contemporary scholars follow this identification. Others, like British New Testament scholar Richard Bauckham, argue that John was actually written by another disciple of Jesus: a young, Jerusalem-based disciple, who was later known as John the Elder.[2] As you may remember from our discussion of Mark, John the Elder was the one who made the connection between Mark and the apostle Peter. In either case, the author of John was a very close disciple of Jesus and an eyewitness to much of what he wrote in his Gospel. He also would have had access to the testimony of other eyewitnesses.

READ JOHN 13:23-25; 19:26; 20:2; 21:7. John referenced an anonymous disciple in all these passages. How did he describe that disciple?

READ JOHN 21:20-24. How did the author reveal in this passage that he is the disciple Jesus loved?

What did this disciple say about his testimony and his book in verse 24?

Perhaps you've heard people claiming that the Gospels of Matthew Mark, Luke, and John were chosen from a larger set of early biographies of Jesus for political reasons and that if we look at other so-called Gospels—like the Gospel of Thomas or the Gospel of Mary—we'll find a very different view of Jesus. But none of these other so-called Gospels were written as early or tied as closely to the actual eyewitnesses of Jesus's life as Matthew, Mark, Luke, and John. Also, rather than offering full biographies of Jesus, they tend to be more like mystical collections of His sayings. If you read them for yourself, you'll find they really can't compete with the Gospels in our Bibles. Even New Testament scholar Bart Ehrman, who is a famous skeptic of the Christian faith, assures us that the four New Testament Gospels are, "the oldest and best sources we have for knowing about the life of Jesus," and that this is "the view of all serious historians of antiquity of every kind, from committed evangelical Christians to hard-core atheists."[3]

We've covered a lot of ground today! Take a few minutes to imagine what it would have been like to be an actual eyewitness of Jesus's life and ministry on earth, or even to talk with people who had been eyewitnesses like the Gospel authors did.

Praise God He's given us not just one but four incredible biographies of Jesus, so that even two-thousand years after His death, we can know so much detail about His life and teachings.

DAY 2

THE EYEWITNESSES

My grandpa was the eldest of seven kids, and he left school at age fourteen so he could work to help support his family. He met my grandma when they were both teenagers, and they married at age twenty. They're now in their eighties. My grandma and grandpa tell many stories from their teens and early twenties, including the story of my mother's birth over sixty years ago. They don't remember everything that happened then, of course. But they remember the highlights.

We saw yesterday that the Gospels were written by people who were either eyewitnesses themselves of Jesus's life or close enough in time to eyewitnesses to gather their testimony. Depending on how old you are, you may be able to remember things from thirty, forty, fifty, or even sixty years ago. But even if you can't, I bet you know people who can!

Today, we'll meet some of the eyewitnesses the Gospel authors point us to. Many of those witnesses traveled with Jesus from place to place, watching His acts and learning His teachings. It was their full-time job. After Jesus's death and resurrection, they spent their time proclaiming what they'd heard and seen. All four Gospels contain testimony of named eyewitnesses, but today, we'll focus in particular on some of the eyewitnesses in Luke's Gospel.

READ LUKE 1:1-3. What did Luke say the original eyewitnesses and servants of the word had done (vv. 1-2)?

What did Luke say he had done (v. 3)?

One of the first eyewitnesses Luke pointed us to is Jesus's mother, Mary. In particular, Luke recorded a private conversation Mary had with an angel, who told her she was going to be the mother of God's own Son (Luke 1:26-38)! Most of the other named witnesses in the first two chapters of Luke—such as Elizabeth, Zechariah, Simeon, or Anna—were already old at the time of Jesus's birth. But Jesus's mother Mary would almost certainly have been a teenager. We know she was still alive after Jesus's death and resurrection (Acts 1:14). So, Luke may have heard Mary's story of meeting the angel from her own lips!

> Have you ever thought about Mary the mother of Jesus as a source of eyewitness testimony for the Gospels? Imagine Mary telling her story of meeting the angel and hearing she'd be the mother of God's Son. How does this change your perspective as you read the beginning of Luke's Gospel?

In Luke 5, Luke introduced us to other named eyewitnesses.

> **READ LUKE 5:3-11.** What are the names of the three fishermen?

> How did Simon Peter react when he saw the miraculous catch of fish (v. 8)?

> What did Jesus tell them they were going to do from now on (v. 10)?

Simon Peter, James, and John went on to become three of Jesus's closest disciples. But Peter's first response to Jesus was to recognize his own sinfulness. Peter knew he had no business being with someone as holy as Jesus! The next disciple we see Jesus call comes from a category of people well known for their sinfulness. He was a tax collector: a Jewish man conspiring with the Roman oppressors and making money off the backs of his fellow Jews.

> **READ LUKE 5:27-28.** How did Levi's response to Jesus's call mirror Peter, James, and John's response in verse 11?

When Jesus chose to select twelve apostles from among His larger group of disciples, Simon Peter, James and John, and Levi—who was also known as Matthew—were among the twelve.

READ LUKE 6:12-16. Write out the list of names and the descriptions Luke gave.

1.   7.

2.   8.

3.   9.

4.   10.

5.   11.

6.   12.

These twelve Jewish apostles mirror the twelve tribes of Israel. When Matthew and Mark listed the apostles in their Gospels, all the names are the same except for Judas son of James. They list "Thaddeus" instead, which was likely a name given to Judas son of James to differentiate him from Judas Iscariot, who betrayed Jesus. (If I had been called Judas, I'd have gone by a different name too!)

Which other names occur twice in the list of Jesus's apostles?

You might have thought that Jesus picking twelve guys with different names would have been less confusing. But the frequency of certain names in the Gospels is evidence of their authenticity. From other texts and records from that period, it seems that Simon was the most common name for Jewish men of Jesus's time and place. Judas was the fourth most common, and James was the eleventh.[4]

Some of the apostles, like Simon Peter, play major roles in the rest of Luke's Gospel. But most of the apostles are never mentioned by name after Luke 6. Nevertheless, being named here makes them important eyewitnesses of Jesus's ministry. In the first chapter of Luke's sequel (the book of Acts), Jesus specifically described them in that way.

READ ACTS 1:8. What did Jesus say His twelve apostles were going to be?

The twelve apostles had an important role. As disciples of Jesus, they would have traveled with Him everywhere to watch what He did and learn what He said. After Jesus's death and resurrection, the apostles traveled around preaching the good news and kick-starting churches. But Luke made it clear these twelve apostles were not Jesus's only disciples. He gave us other named eyewitnesses among that larger group.

READ LUKE 8:1-3. In verses 2 and 3, how did Luke describe the group of women who traveled with Jesus?

What's the name of the first woman Luke highlighted?

Mary was the most common name for Jewish women of that time and place.[5] What additional name did Luke give us for this Mary, and what else did he say about her?

People in that culture didn't have last names like we do. So, this Mary was distinguished from other women named Mary by adding the place she came from: *Magdala*. For similar reasons, Jesus in the Gospels was sometimes called "Jesus of Nazareth."

What's the name of the second woman Luke mentioned?

Joanna was the fifth most common name for Jewish women of that time and place.[6] How is this Joanna distinguished from other women with her same name?

The Herod who was Joanna's husband's boss was not the Herod who was King when Jesus was born but one of his sons, Herod Antipas. Herod Antipas ruled over Galilee during Jesus's public ministry. Chuza's role was an important one in Herod's court, so Joanna would have been a wealthy, well-connected woman.

What is the name of the third woman Luke listed among Jesus's female disciples?

Susanna was a relatively uncommon name, which may be why Luke did not give us any more details to distinguish this Susanna from other women with her name. But Luke listed all three women as eyewitnesses of Jesus's ministry. As we'll see next week, two of them were also eyewitnesses of Jesus's resurrection.

Imagine what it would have been like for these women to follow Jesus as He went through cities and villages preaching and healing. How does it change your view of the Gospels to know the authors relied on the eyewitness testimony of both men and women?

After Luke described Jesus ascending into heaven in the book of Acts (Acts 1:9-11), he once more listed the names of the twelve apostles, minus Judas Iscariot who had betrayed Jesus. Then Luke wrote, "All these with one accord were devoting themselves to prayer, together with the women and Mary the mother of Jesus, and his brothers" (Acts 1:14, ESV). Jesus's male and female disciples, including His mother Mary, were Luke's eyewitness sources for his Gospel account of Jesus's life, death, and resurrection, and they were praying together again after Jesus's ascension! When Luke came to write his Gospel, many of these first eyewitnesses would still have been alive. They'd been telling their stories for decades, and Luke captured their testimony for us!

Praise God that He worked through the lives of individual men and women who knew Jesus well to enable us to learn about His life, death, and resurrection.

Spend some time praying that the Lord would give you the courage to be a witness to Jesus in your own community.

THE DIFFERENCES

It's Saturday morning as I'm sitting at my desk writing this paragraph. My husband is out with the kids for their Saturday morning routine: swimming lessons followed by shopping. They usually have a good time, but last Saturday, everyone came home grumpy. Luke, our three-year-old, was crying. I picked him up and asked him what was wrong. He said, "Daddy was mean." I asked him, "What did Daddy do that was mean?" He replied, "Eliza said Daddy was mean." I interviewed the four eyewitnesses about what had happened in the car on the way home. Apparently, the girls started fighting in the car. Bryan played referee in Miranda's favor, so Eliza was unhappy with him. Luke sided with Eliza, hence his summary: "Daddy was mean." I found common data but four different perspectives.

Yesterday, we met some of the eyewitnesses of Jesus's life and ministry and considered how their testimonies about Jesus shaped the Gospels. But if the Gospels are based on eyewitness testimonies, what are we to make of the times when two Gospels tell the same story but seem to contradict each other? That's the question we'll explore today by looking at one of the most beautiful stories of Jesus's healing power in the Bible. The story is told in Matthew, Mark, and Luke. But we'll focus on Matthew and Mark's accounts.

READ MARK 5:21-43. What details did Mark give us about the man who came to Jesus and the man's request (vv. 22-23)?

What event took place on the way to Jairus's house (vv. 25-34)?

What message arrived for Jairus in verse 35?

How did Jesus respond to the message, and what did He accomplish in the rest of the story (vv. 36-43)?

This is a beautiful story of a double miracle. Maybe you noticed the parallels between the bleeding woman and the dead girl. The woman had been bleeding for twelve years—the same amount of time the girl had been alive. And while the girl was the daughter of the synagogue ruler, the bleeding woman was the only person we ever hear Jesus call "daughter." Mark named the girl's father, Jairus, as an eyewitness to the events. Unlike almost all the other religious leaders we meet in the Gospels, Jairus put his trust in Jesus, the great Healer! But in Matthew's telling of this story, we find a striking difference.

> **READ MATTHEW 9:18-26.** What did the synagogue ruler say about his daughter in verse 18?

> **LOOK BACK AT MARK 5:23.** How is Matthew's account different from Mark's at this point?

Mark's Gospel is the shortest of the four with Mark sometimes telling his stories more concisely. But in this instance, Mark's account is the longer one, with Matthew giving a shorter summary of the action. In Mark's account, Jairus's daughter was sick but still alive when he approached Jesus. Jairus found out she was dead on the way back. But Matthew condensed the story, with Jairus telling Jesus his daughter was dead. We find this kind of thing happening throughout the Gospels. Sometimes, they condense a story. Sometimes, they focus attention on one element of a story to make a particular point.

We see an example of the authors focusing on different elements when Matthew, Mark, and Luke tell the story of a healing miracle as Jesus was on His way out of Jericho. Luke's account is similar to Mark's, but Matthew's account has some notable differences.

> **READ MATTHEW 20:29-34 AND MARK 10:46-52.** Note the differences in the two accounts of the same event, considering the number, names, and dialogue.

Rather than mentioning both blind men, Mark focused on one and told us his name—*Bartimaeus*—because this blind man evidently went on to be an eyewitness of Jesus's ministry. We'll think more about the languages of the Gospels tomorrow, but note that Mark kept the Aramaic word *Rabboni* from Bartimaeus's response, while Matthew gave a Greek equivalent, meaning "Lord." We shouldn't be surprised or concerned by differences like this.

Sometimes, we find similar sounding teachings in the Gospels in different places or with different details. Again, we shouldn't be surprised by this. Jesus spent about three years traveling around and preaching. This was long before the time when you could print books, let alone make audio recordings or post videos on social media of someone teaching! When you think about it, it's obvious that Jesus would have given similar teachings in different towns and villages. The Gospel authors drew from three years' worth of Jesus's sermons. They sought to capture His teaching as best they could in the limited space they had so that future generations of Christians could learn from their Savior. There are teachings that one Gospel author summarized that another Gospel author gave us at greater length. At times, we'll see two Gospel authors drawing from different versions of a sermon, delivered in different places. We can't know for sure.

What's more, sometimes the Gospel authors ordered their material to make a theological point, rather than just ordering it chronologically. For instance, right before Jesus had a run-in with the Pharisees about the Sabbath, Matthew recorded Jesus saying, "Come to me, all of you who are weary and burdened, and I will give you rest. Take up my yoke and learn from me, because I am lowly and humble in heart, and you will find rest for your souls. For my yoke is easy and my burden is light" (Matt. 11:28-30). It's possible Jesus said those words right before that very Sabbath. But it's also very possible Matthew put that teaching immediately before the story that ends with Jesus's claim that He is Lord of the Sabbath (Matt. 12:8).

All the Gospel authors give us faithful access to Jesus's teachings. But like screenplay writers for a biopic, each Gospel author edited down all the possible stories about Jesus he could tell into a narrative that can be read in an hour and a half to two and a half hours. The message across all the Gospels is the same: the God of all the universe became a man and died for us so we could live eternally with Him. We shouldn't be surprised by differences.

DAY 4

THE LANGUAGES

Last Sunday, I was chatting with a young woman who has recently started attending our church. She's from China and is here to do a Ph.D. at Harvard. Christianity is completely new to her, but she's keen to know more and has recently joined our weekly Bible study. As she and I were talking, a friend of mine joined the conversation. This friend was born in China too but moved to the United States when she was a kid. She said, "We can talk in Chinese, if you prefer." I was delighted. Our visitor speaks excellent English, but I was so glad she had the option of exploring Christianity with a mature believer who spoke her mother tongue—especially as it would show that Christianity does not belong to Western culture.

At various times in my life, I've tried to learn a bunch of languages. French. German. Latin. Biblical Hebrew and Greek. But despite years of study, my skills are pretty laughable. I find it deeply impressive that so many of my friends can just switch between two languages as easily as I can turn my bathroom faucet from hot to cold! I can hardly even imagine what it's like to have two languages on the tip of your tongue.

The Bible is a mixture of languages.

The Old Testament was written in Hebrew, with some passages in Aramaic, which became the primary language for Jews of Jesus's time and place. The New Testament is written in Greek, which was the most widely spoken language in the Greco-Roman Empire at the time. Most Christians today can't read any of these languages. So, how can we know that what the Gospels are telling us isn't getting lost in translation?

In today's study, we'll examine the languages we find in the Bible. We'll look at what translation does and doesn't mean when it comes to our ability to access Jesus's actual words, and how understanding more about the languages in the Gospels helps us also think better about some of the differences between them.

READ JOHN 19:19-20. What did the sign on the cross say?

In what three languages was the sign written?

As you probably know, Latin was the language spoken by the ancient Romans. So, writing the charge against Jesus in Latin, Greek, and Aramaic would mean that basically everyone could understand. But what exactly did the sign say?

All four Gospels tell us, but the wording is different in each. Read the four verses listed and write down what each tells us the sign said.

MATTHEW 27:37

MARK 15:26

LUKE 23:38

JOHN 19:19

The basic message on the sign is the same in all four Gospels, but the wording is different. Mark's version—like his Gospel—is the shortest. It's possible that the three different languages had slightly different wording and that each Gospel author chose to translate a different language or combine them. Perhaps the Aramaic sign said, "Jesus of Nazareth" while the Greek sign just said, "Jesus." It's also possible that the Gospel authors summarized the sign in different ways. But the message is the same, and we shouldn't worry about differences like this.

So, did Jesus teach in Greek or Aramaic—or both? We don't know for sure. Sometimes, Jesus's teaching seems specially designed for Greek. For instance, New Testament scholar Peter Williams points out that the first four of Jesus's famous blessings in the Sermon on the Mount all begin with the same Greek letter, suggesting that this teaching was originally delivered in Greek (Matt. 5:3-11).[7] But the Gospels also preserve snatches of Aramaic, showing that Jesus spoke in His mother tongue at least some of the time. We've already come across some words in Aramaic in our study.

REREAD MARK 5:38-41. What two Aramaic words did Jesus say to the dead girl?

Mark translated this into Greek because some of his readers wouldn't have understood Aramaic. Your English Bible translates that Greek into English. What does the English translation say?

NOW READ LUKE 8:54. What did Jesus say to the little girl in Luke's version?

Mark translated what Jesus said in Aramaic with a Greek word meaning *girl* or *young woman*. Luke translated it with a Greek word meaning *child*. Both translations capture the sense of Jesus's words. Knowing that the Gospel authors were probably translating testimonies passed down to them in Aramaic helps us understand why there are some differences between how Jesus's words were recorded in one Gospel versus another. Any time we are translating, we make choices about which words or phrases in one language will be the best equivalents to words or phrases in another. But how do we know that we're not losing a lot in translation between Aramaic and Greek or between the Greek of the Gospels and the English in our Bibles?

In one sense, something is always lost in translation, as there are usually multiple words or phrases in one language that could translate a word or phrase in another. That's why if you open up the same passage in two English Bibles, you'll find some differences. For instance, one of my favorite verses in the Old Testament is Isaiah 49:15.

The New International Version translates it like this:

Can a mother forget the baby at her breast and have no compassion on the child she has borne? Though she may forget, I will not forget you!

And the English Standard Version translates it like this:

> Can a woman forget her nursing child, that she should have no
> compassion on the son of her womb? Even these may forget,
> yet I will not forget you.

Usually—like when Luke picked the Greek word for *child* while Mark picked the
one for *girl*—the English word a translator chooses doesn't change the basic
meaning of the verse. But sometimes it does. So, it can be useful to look at
a couple of different translations to get a sense of the range of possible meanings.
For instance, when Jesus was promising to send the Holy Spirit to His disciples,
the ESV has Jesus call the Holy Spirit "the Helper" while the NIV translates the
same phrase as "the Advocate" and the CSB as "the Counselor." All of them
are valid translations of the Greek word. Some translations (like the ESV) seek to
translate the Greek and Hebrew of the Bible word-for-word, even if that makes
the English version harder to read. Others (like the NLT) translate more thought-
for-thought, seeking to make the Bible more readable for modern audiences,
even if it's less of a word-for-word translation of the original. Some (like the CSB)
seek to find a happy medium between the two. Regardless, we are getting real
access to the Gospels' testimony about Jesus. We don't need to know either
Greek or Aramaic to know that Jesus told that dead little girl to get up!

People sometimes imagine the process of Bible translation involves multiple cycles
over the years, introducing more and more errors. But actually, we have the Greek
texts freely available to refer to if we want to take the time to learn the biblical
languages. Additionally, as more ancient documents have been discovered, our
understanding of the biblical texts and languages has improved to where today's
translations are more accurate than they were even a hundred years ago.

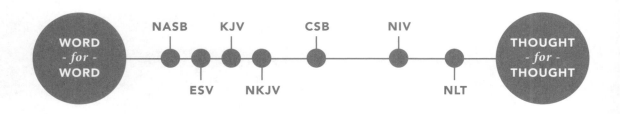

One more thought about how language affects our understanding: As Jesus hung on the cross with the sign above His head, He cried out to God in Aramaic.

READ MARK 15:34. What did Jesus say in Aramaic?

How does your English translation translate Mark's Greek translation?

When Jesus cried out to God from the cross, He quoted the first verse of Psalm 22 in Aramaic: His mother tongue. Nearly two thousand years later, many of us can read this in our own heart language—whether that is English or Chinese, Swahili or Portuguese—thanks to expert scholars doing the work of translation for us. We see the gritty reality of Jesus of Nazareth, the King of the Jews, dying for us, abandoned by God so that we could be welcomed and embraced. That message is proclaimed all around the world today, translated into hundreds of different languages, and currently being translated into even more, so that billions of people can put their trust in Jesus.

For more information on Bible translations, go to csbible.com.

DAY 5

THE TEXTS

My Granny Betty made up comic poems. My favorite went like this:

Wave to the left of us,
Wave to the right of us,
Everyone knows us,
And hates the sight of us!

At least, that's how I remember it. It's possible that instead of "And hates the sight of us" the last line read "They hate the sight of us." Sadly, Granny Betty died four years ago, so I can't check with her. But I could check with her other grandchildren. My cousins live thousands of miles away from me, and we haven't discussed my granny's verse, so their version would be independent of mine. If they all remembered "And," I'd know my version was correct. But if all my seven cousins remembered "They" while my brother and sister said it was "And," I'd assume my immediate family had remembered it wrong. Maybe our dad misremembered it and passed the variant on to us.

When it comes to the texts of the Gospels, we don't have the original, physical manuscripts (or autographs) that Matthew, Mark, Luke, and John wrote. But copies of the Gospels started being made soon after they were written. We actually have many, early Greek manuscripts of all or part of these Gospels. For any given manuscript we have, we can know the approximate date by analyzing the physical material it's written on. The kind of handwriting used is also important, since different ways of writing were used on the biblical manuscripts in different periods. But we don't know whether it was a copy of the autograph, or a copy of a copy, or a copy of a copy of a copy! Manuscripts would typically last 150 to 200 years. So, for example, a copy from the third century could be a copy of the first-century autograph, or a copy of a copy.

The scribes worked very carefully making their copies. But even the most accurate scribe would make occasional mistakes in a long manuscript, and some scribes made intentional changes. So, how can we know what the Gospel authors really wrote? The answer lies in the early spread of Christianity. Because the

Gospels were shared so far and so fast from the very beginning, we have a wealth of early copies that were made independently in different countries. So—like me calling my cousins in England to check what they remember of my Granny's verse— we can compare manuscripts from one place with manuscripts from another and spot mistakes or changes. Experts can look at the family tree of the copies we have and figure out where mistakes crept in. Because we have so many copies of all or part of the Gospels—far more than we have for other ancient manuscripts—the vast majority of the texts of the Gospels are agreed upon.

In the few places where there is doubt that a passage is original, or where we have different, equally authentic-looking versions of a particular verse from different manuscripts, our Bibles will include a note explaining this. One example of this happens at the very beginning of Mark's Gospel.

> **READ MARK 1:1.** What does this verse say about Jesus?

> If you have a footnote in your Bible at the end of this verse, what does it say about the phrase "the Son of God"?

Many early manuscripts leave out the phrase "the Son of God" from Mark 1:1. This might at first seem like a really big deal. Maybe Mark's original just said, "The beginning of the gospel of Jesus Christ," and later Christians added "the Son of God." This seems to back the claim skeptics sometimes make that Jesus was just an inspirational teacher and the idea that He was the Son of God was dreamed up after His death. But let's assume for a minute that Mark didn't write "the Son of God" in the opening sentence of his Gospel. Would that actually support the skeptical argument? No!

> **READ MARK 1:9-11.** How does this passage teach that Jesus is the Son of God?

Even if Mark 1:1 doesn't include "the Son of God," we have plenty of evidence from the rest of his Gospel that Mark was presenting Jesus as the Son of God. Our understanding of that truth does not depend on one verse.

Are there any longer passages in the Gospels that are in doubt? Yes, two. One in John and one in Mark.

READ JOHN 7:53–8:11.

I love this story. It fits beautifully with everything we know about Jesus from the rest of the Gospels, and it may well be a true story, passed down by eyewitnesses and eventually included in copies of John's Gospel. But because it doesn't appear in the earliest copies of John that we have, scholars today think that it was not in John's original autograph. Fortunately, nothing of our understanding of who Jesus is depends on this text. Even if that encounter never happened at all, it wouldn't make a difference to Christian belief.

But what about the ending of Mark's Gospel?

If you open your Bible to Mark 16:9-20, you'll likely find a note telling you that some of the earliest manuscripts of Mark do not include these verses. If you read through them, you may notice that they summarize some stories told in other Gospels. As we'll see next week, at first glance, verse 8 seems to leave the story hanging, so it's understandable that people might have wanted to add a conclusion based on other writings about Jesus. But again, nothing of our understanding of who Jesus is depends on verses 9-20.

What's more, if we were to examine all of the texts in the Gospels where there is any significant doubt as to which version of the text is original (most of which are very short) it wouldn't make any real difference to our understanding of who Jesus is. In his excellent discussion of these issues, New Testament scholar William D. Mounce points out that even Bart Ehrman—the most famous current critic of the New Testament—agrees with this analysis.[8]

But even if the few questionable verses or passages in the Gospels don't change our view of Jesus, do they change our view of Scripture? As a Christian, I believe the entire Bible is inspired by God and totally trustworthy. But we need to understand that Christians believe the Bible is inspired by God in its original form and languages. So, the original autographs written by Matthew, Mark, Luke, and John were inspired by the Spirit. But thankfully, so many copies of these originals were made that we can be confident that the texts in our Bibles today are very, very close to what Matthew, Mark, Luke, and John originally wrote. What's more, many scholars have invested lifetimes of research to translate the Gospels for us into English, so while individual English translations do not come with a guarantee of divine inspiration, we can be confident we're getting the accurate message about Jesus.

REFLECT

What new things have you learned about the Gospels in our studies this week?

After examining the Gospels more closely, do you feel more or less confident that the Gospels are giving us access to Jesus?

What remaining questions do you have?

SESSION TWO

Narrative

As we saw last week, the Gospel authors are trustworthy biographers, but they're not dry historians: they're storytellers. Matthew, Mark, Luke, and John are eager to tell us the truth about Jesus but also to persuade us. They want us to know Him and leave everything to follow him. If you sat down with the Gospel authors and said, "I hate to tell you this, but I think you're biased toward Jesus," they'd say, "Too right I am! He's the rightful King of all the universe, and yet He loved me so much he came to die for me!"

Their bias doesn't mean they're making things up. There was no need for that. As John wrote toward the end of his Gospel, "Jesus performed many other signs in the presence of his disciples that are not written in this book. But these are written so that you may believe that Jesus is the Messiah, the Son of God, and that by believing you may have life in his name" (John 20:30-31). When we read narrative, we need to remember that the Gospel authors are being highly selective in what they have space to say, so they're using every strategy at their disposal to communicate with us. This means every detail counts. It also means that one Gospel author might leave out some details included by a different Gospel author because he's summarizing or making a different point. It also shows that the way the Gospel authors organize their material is part of how they communicate.

With this understanding in place, we're going to spend our time this week looking at some of the most important narratives in all of the Gospels: the four accounts of Jesus's resurrection. Each day, we'll look at the resurrection story in a different Gospel, splitting John's Gospel over days 4 and 5. Examining the four resurrection accounts will showcase how each Gospel author tells us stories from his own particular angle, with the purpose not just of informing us about the things that Jesus did but of persuading us that Jesus is the Son of God, that by believing we may have life in His name.

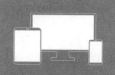

SESSION Two

To access the video teaching sessions, use the instructions in the back of your Bible study book.

Jesus Has Dinner w/ women who poured expensive ointment

NOTES

Watch Rebecca's Session Two video.

- Gospels are written for us to believe that Christ is the son of God & that in believing in this we can have life through Christ

1. The People
   - named individuals, unamed, groups
   - simon the leper - host of dinner
   - anonymous women - pours ointment on Jesus - just b/c anonymous, doesnt mean less significant
   - groups - can work together & make public statement through one person

2. The Place
   - named or described

3. The Plot
   - moves us toward Jesus death & ressurection

4. The Position!
   - intentional

Download the *Navigating Gospel Truth* leader guide at lifeway.com/gospeltruth

GROUP DISCUSSION GUIDE

What is the purpose of narratives in the Gospels?

- r

How can you explain why there are differences in some of the Gospel narratives?

organized in a way for us to see different things through one story

When you consider people, place, plot, and position, which do you consider most important when it comes to determining the purpose of narrative in the Gospels? Why?

The Position-organizing story in different ways can convey diff messages

Why is it important for you to understand the purpose of narrative in the Gospels?

so you can really believe in Christ & fully understand purpose of Gospel

What part of the video teaching was most important for you?

The plot — no matter how it differs its always moving us toward Jesus death & ressurection

BIBLICAL PARALLEL

This week, we'll be looking at the resurrection story from all four Gospels. Fill out this chart before you begin your week of personal study. This will give you an overall view that you can refer to during the week.

	MATTHEW 28:1-10	MARK 16:1-8	LUKE 24:1-12	JOHN 20:1-18
1. Who were the women that went to the tomb?	· Mary Magdelene - Mary	- Mary Magdeline - Mary, mother of James - Salome	- unamed women	- Mary M.
2. Whom did they see and how many?	- one angel	- one young man	- two men	· N/A
3. What did the angel(s) initially say to them?	Do not be afraid for I know that you are looking for Jesus, who was crucified	Dont be alarmed, you were looking for Jesus the Nazarene who was crucified. He has risen	why do you look for the living among the dead	-N/A

	MATTHEW 28:1-10	MARK 16:1-8	LUKE 24:1-12	JOHN 20:1-18
4. What instructions did the angels give?	- go to where he layed - go tell tell disip'ls He has risen & is going to Gaililee which is where you will see him	- see place where they laid him - tell disiples & peter He is going to Galilee & you will see him there	No instructions	- N/A
5. What was the women's response?	- hurried away from tomb	- trembling & be wildered - went out & fled tomb - said nothing to anyone b/c they were afraid	- told experience to eleven disciples & Mary M, Joanna, Mary	- ran to Simon, peur & other disciple - brought them to tomb
6. Did the women encounter Jesus? If so, what happened?	- Jesus met them - they clasped his feet & worshipped him - instructed them to continue what angel said.	NO	NO	- NO

DAY 1

THE WOMEN

The #metoo mantra "Believe women" would not have gone down well in the first century. In the Greco-Roman Empire, women were seen as inferior to men, and their testimonies were often discounted. For example, the first-century Jewish-Roman historian Josephus wrote, "Let not the testimony of women be admitted, on account of the levity and boldness of their sex."[1] So, if you were making up a story in the first century and wanted people to believe it, the last thing you'd do is tell them that a group of women saw what happened! But all four Gospels point us to the testimony of women when it comes to Jesus's resurrection. In our study today, we're going to look at who these women were and what we can learn from them about how the Gospel authors shaped their narratives.

READ MARK 16:1-8. What did the women do when the Sabbath was over? Why?

- brought spices so that they might annoint Jesus

The Sabbath ran from Friday sundown to Saturday sundown, at which point stores would reopen. So, it seems the women bought spices to anoint Jesus's body on Saturday evening and then planned to visit His tomb at first light on Sunday morning.

Which three women did Mark name?

Mary M., Salome, Mary

Mark named the same three women as witnesses of Jesus's crucifixion.

READ MARK 15:40-41. What extra information did Mark give us here about these women? *- followed Jesus & cared for him*

Mary ~~mother of James~~
mary = mother of James & Joseph

How does this extra information help us imagine how they felt as they went to Jesus's tomb so early that Sunday morning?

They felt hopeful & a lot of care towards Jesus

Mark also stated that two of these women were watching when Jesus was buried: "Mary Magdalene and Mary the mother of Joses were watching where he was laid" (v. 47).

Why do you think Mark included this detail?

To git credibility of their witness to His burial

In Mark 16:3, what were the women wondering about on their way to the tomb? *who will roll the stone away*

Look back at the chart on pages 40–41 and summarize the women's experience at the tomb.

As we saw in Session One, Day Five, verse 8 was likely the original ending of Mark. How can we make sense of this, given that all the other Gospels say the women did tell the apostles?

One of my favorite New Testament scholars, Richard Bauckham, argues that Mark clearly didn't mean that the women never told *anyone* what they'd seen. In fact, the presence of their testimony in Mark's Gospel proves they did! It especially suggests they told Peter, as Mark's Gospel is based on Peter's memories. Bauckham argues that what Mark meant is that the women didn't tell anyone other than the apostles as they'd been instructed. Bauckham also points out the women's fear and trembling is not evidence of their cowardice but rather the appropriate response to what they saw and heard.[2] The message of the resurrected Son of God is absolutely terrifying news!

In fact, if we look back through Mark's whole narrative, we'll find that fear has been a consistent response to Jesus's power. The disciples were afraid when Jesus calmed a storm (Mark 4:39-41) and when they saw Him walking on water (Mark 6:49-51). People were afraid when Jesus healed a demon-possessed man by sending the unclean spirits into a herd of pigs (Mark 5:15), and the bleeding woman whom Jesus healed was trembling and afraid when she fell at Jesus's feet (Mark 5:33). Peter, James, and John were afraid when they saw Jesus suddenly transfigured on a mountain top (Mark 9:2-6), and the disciples were afraid when Jesus predicted His death and resurrection for the second time (Mark 9:30-32). Of course, the women were afraid when they discovered that Jesus had been raised from the dead!

While Mark didn't tell us about the women passing on the news, he did present them clearly as eyewitnesses. First-century historians placed a lot of importance on what people saw.

Work through Mark 16:1-8 and note all the ways in which the women are described as seeing things in the following verses:

Verse 4 (note: the word translated "noticed" is also a seeing word in the Greek)[3]

- look up, saw that stone

Verse 5

- saw young man

Verse 6

looking for Jesus

Verse 7

you will see him

Mark used multiple Greek verbs to highlight the women's role as eyewitnesses. Eyewitnesses also needed to hear and to speak.

Work through Mark 16:1-8 again and write down all the references to speaking in the following verses:

Verse 3

- asked eachother

Verse 6

Verse 7
tell His disciples

Verse 8
said nothing

We tend to think most stories build to a climax at the end. However, biblical narratives often put the most important message in the middle, with the beginning and the end of the story pairing with each other. We see correspondence in Mark's passage between verses 1-3 at the beginning when the women go to the tomb and talk to each other, and in verse 8 when the women run away from the tomb and say nothing to anyone.

What is the vital message in the middle of Mark's story?

They are eyewitnesses

As we've seen, Mark was clearly presenting Mary Magdalene, Mary the mother of James, and Salome as eyewitnesses of Jesus's empty tomb. But if we read the resurrection accounts in Matthew, Luke, and John, we find discrepancies between the lists of women mentioned.

Write down the names of women in each of the Gospel accounts:

CRUCIFIXION	Matthew 27:56	Mark 15:40-41	Luke 23:49	John 19:25
NAMES	- Mary M - Mary - Mother of Zebedee's sons	Mary M, Mary, Salome - other women	- the women	- Jesus mother - mothers sister, - Mary - Mary M
RESURRECTION	Matthew 28:1	Mark 16:1	Luke 24:10	John 20:1
NAMES	- Mary M - Mary	- Mary M - Mary - Salome	- Mary M, Joanna Mary	- Mary M.

Which woman appears in all four Gospels?

- Mary M.

Skeptical New Testament scholar Bart Ehrman argues that these differences point to confusion and contradiction between the Gospels.

"Who actually went to the tomb?" he asks, "Was it Mary alone (John 20:1)? Mary and another Mary (Matthew 28:1)? Mary Magdalene, Mary the mother of James, and Salome (Mark 16:1)? Or women who had accompanied Jesus from Galilee to Jerusalem—possibly Mary Magdalene, Joanna, Mary the mother of James, and "other women" (Luke 24:1; see 23:55)?"[4]

But this analysis shows a misunderstanding of the purpose of the names. The Gospel authors weren't offering a comprehensive list; they were naming the eyewitnesses they wanted to highlight. For example, when Mark named three women who were witnesses of Jesus's crucifixion, he made it clear that there were other women there as well (Mark 15:40-41). Likewise, even though John only named Mary Magdalene, it's also clear in his narrative that there were other women with her, as she spoke in the plural (John 20:2).

We've seen today that narrative in the Gospels is based on eyewitness testimony, that different Gospel authors drew on different eyewitnesses, and that they're telling it like it is. That included naming women as the witnesses of the resurrection when naming men would have been more persuasive to their first readers. We've also seen that the Gospel authors often shaped their narratives so that the beginning mirrors the end, and the most important message is in the middle.

The Gospel authors weren't inventing myths. They were writing history. But they shaped their narratives to help us better understand who Jesus is and how we should respond to Him.

> Take some time to reflect on what the women in Mark saw and heard. How does their fear and trembling response to the news of Jesus's resurrection help us see how incredible and awe-inspiring Jesus's resurrection really is?

Helps me try to comprehend what I would have done

DAY 2

THE ANGELS

When people ask me how I met my husband, Bryan, I sometimes say, "At church." Other times, I tell them we met at a Saint Patrick's Day party. Still other times, I say we met at Cambridge University. All three answers are true. You see, we knew each other slightly from church because we were both serving on a team that led the weekly student Bible studies. But there were lots of people on the team, so we only really knew each other's names. Then, one Saint Patrick's Day, my college had an exchange dinner with his college. When I walked into the dining hall with my friends, I spotted him. I said, "I know that guy from church. Let's sit with him!" It was the first time we had really talked. It wasn't love at first bite of that dinner. Our journey was a complex one. But somehow, we got married in the end, and fifteen years later, we're both happy we did!

Today, we're going to read Matthew's account of the women's visit to the empty tomb, and we're going to compare what Matthew says about whom they met there to what the other Gospel authors say. But first, let's read Matthew's unique narrative about what happened on Saturday, the day after Jesus was buried.

READ MATTHEW 27:62-66. What did the chief priests and Pharisees call Pilate, the Roman governor, in verse 63?

How did the chief priests and Pharisees refer to Jesus in verse 63, and what teaching of His did they recall?

What did they request of Pilate? Why?

What two things did the chief priests and Pharisees do to secure Jesus's tomb in verse 66?

Sealing the tomb likely meant placing a wax seal between the stone that was rolled over the entrance and the edge of the tomb itself. Only an authorized agent could legally break the seal. The Jewish leaders and the Roman authorities had been in league together to have Jesus crucified. Now, they'd teamed up to make sure His body stayed in His tomb. But on the next day, Sunday, two women who had watched Jesus being crucified (Matt. 27:56) and who had watched Him being buried (Matt. 27:61) came to see Jesus's tomb again.

READ MATTHEW 28:1-8. What details did Matthew give about how the stone was rolled away?

In Mark's account, the women "saw a young man dressed in a white robe" (Mark 16:5). How did Matthew describe this same figure?

We tend to think of angels as having wings and it being obvious they are supernatural beings. But while angels in the Bible can be super scary, they're confused for humans on multiple occasions (for example, Gen. 18:1-2; Josh. 5:13-14). So, when Mark said the women saw a young man in white but Matthew said they saw an angel of the Lord, they were not contradicting each other.

The young man in Mark told the women not to be afraid (Mark 16:6), but Matthew doubled down on the power and scariness of the angel.

Why do you think Matthew emphasized the power and frightening aspects of the angel, given the other details of the story he included?

The Greek word *angelos* means messenger, and we see the angels at Jesus's tomb acting as messengers to the women.[5] But angels in the Bible are also supernatural warriors; Matthew's narrative draws out this aspect. The Jewish and Roman leaders did their best to keep the stone on Jesus's tomb. But they didn't stand a chance against an angel of the Lord!

If we compare the different resurrection accounts, we'll find some sort of messenger in each. But we'll also notice differences. Review your chart on pages 40–41 and fill out this table with the details from each Gospel account.

	ANGEL(S)	MAN/MEN
ONE	Matthew 28:2-3	Mark 16:5
TWO	John 20:12	Luke 24:4

Does this mean Matthew and Mark were wrong when they said there was only one man/angel? No. Just as John's Gospel focuses our attention on Mary Magdalene's visit to the empty tomb, despite there being other women there as well, so Matthew and Mark focus on one angel. We make narrative choices like this in our normal lives.

Last week, I got to catch up with one of my closest friends. It had been a while since we'd had an opportunity to talk one-on-one. So when I came home, I told Bryan, "I got to see Julie by herself today for the first time in ages!" He asked, "Where were the kids?" I said, "Oh, they were there too." Julie has four kids.

I have three. Most of the time Julie and I have spent together, we've had our seven kids in tow. When I said I got to see Julie "by herself" I meant, "without another adult." If my daughter Eliza had been telling the story, she'd mostly have talked about Julie's eldest daughter, Lydia, who is one of her best friends. My son, Luke, would have talked about their new trampoline. Likewise, when we come to narrative in the Gospels, we should expect to see different perspectives on the same story and pay attention to what each Gospel author highlights.

> How would you respond to a friend who said she couldn't believe the resurrection account in the Gospels because the Gospel authors disagree about whether there was one angel or two, and whether they were angels or just men in white?

Matthew also included in his resurrection account a brief summary of Mary Magdalene and Mary the mother of James and Joseph's meeting with Jesus Himself. (We'll compare what Matthew says with John's account on Day Five.)

> READ MATTHEW 28:8-10. How did the women's reaction to Jesus show that they finally really understood who He is?

> How did Jesus's message to the Marys echo what the angel said?

As we saw on Day One, the Gospel authors often end a narrative with something that brings back ideas from the beginning of the narrative, with the most important part of the story sandwiched in the middle.

READ MATTHEW 28:11-15. How does this passage connect back to Matthew 27:62-66?

Now, let's see how Matthew ended his Gospel as a whole.

READ MATTHEW 28:16-20. How does this passage contrast with verses 11-15?

How does it connect back to verses 1-10?

How does Jesus's claim in verse 18 present Him as more powerful than both the Roman and the Jewish authorities?

How does Jesus's resurrection prove He really does have all authority in heaven and on earth?

What difference does that make to us today?

Matthew's resurrection narrative highlights the ways in which Jesus's resurrection demonstrates His power and authority. The One who died a seemingly humiliating death turns out to be the universal Lord of all in heaven and on earth. While angels may be scary, they are only servants of the Lord. While human kings and emperors and presidents and rulers of all kinds may seem to hold the power in our world, their power is nothing in comparison to Jesus's power, as the One who conquered even death itself. Let's share His message with the world!

THE MESSAGE

One of my favorite Shakespeare plays, *Romeo and Juliet*, hinges on a failure of the mail! You may remember the story. Romeo and Juliet fall in love and marry in secret because their families hate each other. But then Romeo gets banished from Verona for revenge-killing Juliet's cousin. Meanwhile, Juliet's parents are forcing her to marry a guy named Paris. But Friar Lawrence, who married her to Romeo in the first place, comes up with a plan. He's going to give Juliet a potion that will make it seem like she's dead when she's actually just deeply asleep. Her parents will put her in her tomb, and she'll keep sleeping for a while. In the meantime, Friar Lawrence will write to Romeo and fill him in on the plan so Romeo can come and steal her away. Bingo! Happy ending. Except the message doesn't get to Romeo in time. Instead, he hears that Juliet is dead, goes to her tomb, and kills himself. She wakes up to find Romeo dead and kills herself as well. All this because a letter didn't make it!

In the Gospel accounts of Jesus's resurrection, God didn't write a letter to the disciples to explain what happened. Instead, He sent angels. Today, we're going to look at Luke's account of the resurrection, specifically noting what the angels said, and then compare it with the other Gospels. This will help us understand how the Gospel authors thought about reporting conversations. Just as with other elements of narrative, their aim was not to be exhaustive but instructive.

READ LUKE 24:1-12. What question did the angels ask the women?

What did the angels say about Jesus?

Why do you think the angels pointed back to what Jesus had said to His followers about His death and resurrection?

If we compare the message in Luke's Gospel with what we saw in Matthew and Mark's accounts, we'll notice both similarities and differences.

Look back at the chart on pages 40–41 to note the similarities and the differences between the three messages.

How can we explain the differences between the three accounts of what the angel(s) said?

First, as we've already noted, the Gospel authors were selective. Just as they didn't give us every detail of a story, they didn't give us every word of every conversation they reported. Rather, they highlighted what they wanted to emphasize.

Second, just as we sometimes summarize what people have said, so the Gospel authors sometimes gave us a faithful summary of what the eyewitnesses heard. Last week, I went out for dinner with two close friends: Julie and Lexi. We talked for two hours straight. The next morning, I texted our mutual friend Rachel with a summary of the conversation, because it touched on things that she and I had talked about recently as well. Of course, the text message I sent to Rachel wasn't a transcript of my whole conversation with our other friends. But if I'd shown it to Julie and Lexi, they would have agreed it was a faithful summary. Likewise, while Luke reported the angels saying, "He is not here, but he has risen! Remember how he spoke to you when he was still in Galilee, saying, 'It is necessary that the Son of Man be betrayed into the hands of sinful men, be crucified, and rise on the third day'?" Matthew gives a briefer summary: "He is not here. For he has risen, just as he said" (Matt. 28:6).

Third, as we saw last week, the Gospels were all written in Greek. But Jesus's Jewish disciples likely spoke Aramaic as their mother tongue. It's very possible that the angels spoke to the women in Aramaic and the message was translated into Greek when it was written down. So, differences in wording should not trouble us. The purpose of the Gospels is not to give us a transcript of Jesus's life on earth. It's to give us faithful testimony.

> Think of a time when you gave a summary of a conversation to someone who wasn't part of it. How much detail did you leave out? How would you have summarized differently if you were telling it to someone else—for example, someone you were meeting for the first time versus someone who already knew you well?

> What's the difference between a faithful summary that leaves a lot out and an unfaithful summary that misrepresents the conversation?

> In Luke 24:8, the women remembered what Jesus had taught them about His death and resurrection. What did they do in verse 9?

Luke saved his listing of the women until this point in the narrative. Two of the three women he mentioned—Mary Magdalene and Joanna—were in the original list of women whom he named as eyewitnesses of Jesus's ministry in Luke 8:1-3. As the wife of Herod's steward, Joanna would have been part of the court of Herod Antipas, the king who mocked and abused Jesus before His crucifixion (Luke 23:6-16). She must have taken a massive risk to leave Herod's court and follow Jesus all the way to the cross and to the empty tomb!

> How did the eleven remaining apostles and the other disciples react to the women's message in Luke 24:11?

How did Peter react in verse 12?

This is an embarrassing episode for the apostles. They should have believed these women, who had traveled with them for years. But they didn't. Two of them got specifically rebuked for this by Jesus when He appeared to them later that same day.

READ LUKE 24:13-35. How did Jesus rebuke these two disciples, and how did He follow up His rebuke (vv. 25-27)?

If you read through the rest of Luke 24, you'll notice a twin emphasis.

First, Luke emphasized that Jesus was physically raised from the dead.

Write down the evidence for this in the following verses:

Verses 39-40

Verses 41-43

Second, Luke emphasized that Jesus's death and resurrection fulfilled both the Scriptures and Jesus's own words.

Write down the evidence for this in the following verses:

Verse 44

Verses 45-48

How does this twin emphasis reinforce the message the women first heard from the angel in verses 5-7?

We saw yesterday that Matthew's distinctive emphasis in his resurrection account was on Jesus's victory over the powers and authorities that were against Him. We've seen today that Luke's distinctive emphasis was on the way that Jesus's bodily resurrection fulfills the Scriptures and Jesus's own words.

How has Luke's narrative helped you to see the importance of Jesus's physical resurrection?

How has it helped you to see that Jesus's death and resurrection were always God's salvation plan?

DAY 4

THE LORD

Have you ever been mocked for your faith? I have. It never really hurt my feelings because I was used to being different, but I remember times in high school and college when people would laugh at me for taking the Bible so seriously. It's nothing new. Christians have been laughed at from the beginning. But the reasons for ridicule have changed over the years. In the second century AD, a Greek philosopher named Celsus mocked Christianity as a religion of women, slaves, and little children. This caricature was grounded in truth. Christianity was especially popular with women and slaves. But to Celsus it made total sense: only uneducated and foolish people could possibly believe this tale of a crucified man who rose from the dead and was claimed to be the universal Lord of all! What's more, Celsus thought it was ridiculous that a weeping woman was central to the accounts of Jesus's resurrection: "after death [Jesus] rose again and showed the marks of his punishment and how his hands had been pierced," he observed, "But who saw this? A hysterical female, as you say, and perhaps some other one of those who were deluded by the same sorcery."[6]

As we noted in Day One, Mary Magdalene was named as a witness of the resurrection by all four Gospel authors. But in John's Gospel, she is the particular focus. Not only did she see the empty tomb and the angels, she also met Jesus Himself.

John is the only Gospel author who directly claims to have been an eyewitness of Jesus's life on earth, including witnessing Jesus's crucifixion (John 19:26). But he nonetheless cited three women as witnesses of the crucifixion, including Jesus's own mother:

> Standing by the cross of Jesus were his mother, his mother's sister, Mary the wife of Clopas, and Mary Magdalene.

JOHN 19:25

Clopas seems to have been a brother of Joseph, so Mary the wife of Clopas was very likely the sister-in-law of Mary the mother of Jesus.

What do you notice about all three of the women whom John names as witnesses of Jesus's crucifixion?

Yes, there are a lot of Marys! In fact, across the Gospels, we see four Marys named as witnesses in the accounts of Jesus's death, burial, and resurrection. If you were making up a story, it would be super weird to call so many women Mary. Seriously. Four Marys? But it makes perfect sense for the particular community of first-century Jews in which Jesus lived, since sources suggest that one woman in five was named Mary. In fact, this is one of many ways in which the Gospel accounts of Jesus's life align with evidence we have about the society in which He lived.

One of my best friends from seminary comes from Kenya. His name is Kiprotich—or Kip for short—and it means *boy, born in the late afternoon*. You see, in his tribe, children are named according to their sex and the time of day when they were born. If someone was claiming to report on events that had happened in the exact place where Kip grew up but didn't use the right names, Kip would laugh out loud. But if the narrative contained the right kinds of names and involved the right kind of food and customs and geography, it would be clear that the author either came from that place or had talked to people from that exact region. As scholars have learned more and more about the exact time and place where Jesus lived on earth, they've found a host of ways in which the Gospel stories match up with the local names and foods and customs.

READ JOHN 20:1-13. What did Mary Magdalene do when she saw the stone had been rolled away from Jesus's tomb?

As we saw in Session One, the author of John's Gospel referred to himself as "the one [disciple] Jesus loved" (John 13:23). This doesn't mean Jesus loved him more than the other disciples. (Check out John 11:5 to see the same language applied to three siblings: Mary, Martha, and Lazarus.) It was just John's way of talking about himself. Perhaps it was his way of saying being loved by Jesus was the most important thing in his life.

> What did the apostles Peter and John do when they heard Mary Magdalene's news?

> Did Peter and John understand what they were seeing at the tomb?

> Whom did Mary see after Peter and John left? Describe their conversation.

John left out everything that Matthew, Mark, and Luke reported about the angels' conversation with Mary Magdalene! They just asked her one question.

> **READ JOHN 20:14-18.** Whom did Mary Magdalene see, and what mistake did she make?

> What did Jesus ask her, and how does it compare with what the angels asked her?

Calling someone "woman" in that culture would not have been rude. Jesus called His mother "woman" twice in John's Gospel. It had different connotations from calling someone "girl" in American culture today but could likewise be a friendly mode of address.

> At first, surprisingly, Mary didn't recognize Jesus. What happened that caused her to recognize Him?

The reason Mary didn't recognize Jesus immediately is not given. It could have been that her grief and tears clouded her vision. Or perhaps she was just prevented from recognizing Him at first. We don't know. But what we do know from the text is that when Jesus called Mary Magdalene by her very common name, she recognized Him—even through her tears.

What does this encounter communicate about Jesus's personal love for His followers?

Mary responded in Aramaic—"*Rabboni!*" John told us this means "Teacher." Mary was a disciple, and Jesus was her Rabbi. She immediately grabbed hold of Him: "'Don't cling to me,' Jesus told her, 'since I have not yet ascended to the Father. But go to my brothers and tell them that I am ascending to my Father and your Father, to my God and your God'" (v. 17). Jesus told Mary that their relationship was changing and that He now had a job for her to do. Mary Magdalene was to be the first messenger of the good news about the risen Jesus.

People sometimes claim that Jesus was just a good teacher. How does this passage help us understand that Jesus's identity as teacher cannot be separated from His identity as the resurrected Lord of all?

When we compare John's account with Matthew's, we find that Mary Magdalene had grabbed hold of Jesus's feet and worshiped Him (Matt. 28:8-10). She knew this was the only right response to the risen Lord. But once she recognized who Jesus was, she found He had work for her to do. John tells us that "Mary Magdalene went and announced to the disciples, 'I have seen the Lord!' And she told them what he had said to her" (John 20:18).

How hard is it for you to believe that Jesus knows you by name, just as He knew Mary Magdalene?

Why do you think John focused on Mary Magdalene's story?

DAY 5

THE EVIDENCE

Do you have a nickname? I've picked up several over the years. Perhaps the most memorable is one I had when I was playing soccer (which in England is called *football*) for my college team. My maiden name was Beale, which led to the moniker "Becca Beale made of steel." I'm not sure it was a compliment! As we've already seen, several of Jesus's first disciples had common names and ended up with nicknames. For example, when Jesus first met Simon, He said, "'You are Simon, son of John. You will be called Cephas' (which is translated 'Peter')" (John 1:42), and Mary Magdalene was named for the town of Magdala, where she came from. But one of Jesus's disciples has been given a nickname by Christians long after the disciple's death: doubting Thomas. We'll find out why in our study today.

READ JOHN 20:19-23. John described Jesus's meeting with Mary Magdalene on Sunday morning. According to these verses, describe what happened on Sunday evening.

How did Jesus's words and actions described in verses 21-22 fulfill what John the Baptist said about Jesus in John 1:33?

What strange claim did Jesus make in John 20:23?

Jesus commissioned His disciples and prepared their hearts to receive the Holy Spirit. He talked about the forgiveness that comes when the message of the gospel is applied by the Holy Spirit and people repent and believe. The disciples now had all they needed to take forgiveness out into the world. But anyone who does not respond does not receive forgiveness. John went on to show us one person's response.

READ JOHN 20:24-29. In this passage, we see the disciples' first attempt at sharing the good news of Jesus's resurrection.

What message did the other disciples give Thomas, and how did Thomas respond (v. 25)?

How did Jesus confront Thomas, and how did Thomas respond in verses 27-28?

How is this the appropriate response to the resurrected Jesus?

How do Jesus's words in verse 29 welcome people like us, who are not eyewitnesses of His resurrection, onto His team?

READ JOHN 20:30-31. What do we learn about the scope and purpose of John's Gospel from these verses?

If you and I sat down together and shared our life stories, we'd have to leave out much more than we included. We'd also likely tell the story differently depending on who we were talking to, how long we had to share, or what we thought might interest them. When Matthew, Mark, Luke, and John sat down to write their accounts of Jesus's resurrection, they weren't setting out to write a blow-by-blow account of that first Easter morning. They each made their own director's cut to help us see who Jesus is.

READ JOHN 21:24-25. How did John end his Gospel? Why do you think he ended it this way?

John ended his Gospel with these words: "there are also many other things that Jesus did, which, if every one of them were written down, I suppose not even the world itself could contain the books that would be written" (v. 25). So, when we read the narratives the Gospel authors do include, we know that every sentence counts. As John put it, "these are written so that you may believe that Jesus is the Messiah, the Son of God, and that by believing you may have life in his name" (John 20:31).

What has struck you most from reading the different resurrection accounts side-by-side this week?

Do you feel better equipped to read and understand the narrative portions of the Gospels? Explain.

Whom do you most identify with in the resurrection accounts and why?

What are your biggest takeaways from our study of narrative in the Gospels?

READING NARRATIVE WELL

IN THE GOSPELS >

This week, we looked at the resurrection stories in each of the Gospels to better understand the narrative portions of the Gospels. We've seen how the Gospel writers told their stories differently and why. As you continue to read the narrative portions of the Gospels, here are some things to keep in mind:

> The Gospel authors were being highly selective, both in the stories they told and which details they did and didn't include.

> Stories are sometimes ordered theologically (to make a point) rather than chronologically.

> Gospel authors were often summarizing conversations or highlighting different pieces of what someone said, so we shouldn't be surprised by differences in dialogue.

> As a traveling rabbi, Jesus taught similar things in different places and at different times. If we see a similar but not identical teaching in two Gospels, we shouldn't be surprised.

> Jews of Jesus's time and place mostly spoke Aramaic, but the Gospels were written in Greek, so different authors may have made different translation decisions.

> Matthew, Luke, and John very likely had access to Mark's Gospel or at least parts of it. They're adding to his testimony rather than contradicting it.

Exercise

The story of Jesus feeding the five thousand is the only miracle story told by each Gospel author. Read each account and note similarities, differences, and thoughts about what you learn from reading this narrative well.

MATTHEW 14:13-21; MARK 6:31-44; LUKE 9:10-17; JOHN 6:1-14		
SIMILARITIES	DIFFERENCES	THOUGHTS

Metaphor

D*o you take the Bible literally?*

My guess is we've all been asked that question—or maybe we've asked it ourselves. What people usually mean by it is, "Are you one of those crazy people who really believes what the Bible says?" But if you read through even one book of the Bible, you'll likely notice that it often speaks to us in non-literal ways. Recognizing this does not mean we're watering God's Word down or sloughing off the hard truths we don't want to hear. In fact, God delivers some of His hardest and most painful messages through non-literal language. This week, we'll focus on one form of non-literal communication which we find throughout the Bible: *metaphor.*

So, what exactly is a metaphor? At a basic level, a metaphor compares two different things. Unlike a simile, when the comparison is pointed out—for example, "My love is like a fire in my bones"—a metaphor just goes for the gold: for example, "My love is a fire in my bones." Like someone used to driving a stick shift and automatically changing gears, we're so used to navigating metaphors that we often don't even notice what we're doing.

Think about your favorite song. Most likely, it's shot through with metaphors. I just did a Google® search and found that one of the most listened-to songs this week is, "Easy on Me" by Adele. The whole first verse of that song depends on water metaphors. Adele says she can't bring herself to swim when she's drowning in this silence. We all know you can't literally drown in silence. But we totally get what she means. If someone told you that was how he felt, you wouldn't say, "That's not true: you can't drown in silence." Instead, you'd feel his pain.

People use metaphors in songs and poems and even in everyday conversations because they speak to our hearts and draw us in. The Bible uses metaphors for that reason too. But biblical metaphors run even deeper than our own. Adele looks at water, notices the ways it can be used—for washing, drinking, swimming, drowning—and uses those things to express how she is feeling. But God made water in the first place in part so He could call Himself "the fountain of living water" (Jer. 2:13) and we would understand a little more of who He is.

This week, we'll look at five metaphors we find in the Gospels. We'll see that metaphors communicate some of the most amazing claims about God and some of the hardest teachings. We'll also see how Jesus tapped into Old Testament metaphors to help us see the truth of who He is.

SESSION *Three*

To access the video teaching sessions, use the instructions in the back of your Bible study book.

NOTES

Watch Rebecca's Session Three video.

Download the *Navigating Gospel Truth* leader guide at lifeway.com/gospeltruth

GROUP DISCUSSION GUIDE

What is a metaphor?

What are some examples of how the Gospel writers used metaphors?

Gospel metaphors speak truth, fulfill Scripture, shape reality, and woo hearts. Which is most significant to you? Why?

Why is it important to understand how metaphors are used in the Gospels?

What part of the video teaching was most important for you?

DAY 1

THE FATHER

My best friend, Rachel, was ten when her parents told her that her dad was not her biological father. The man whose genes she carried had abused her and her mother when Rachel was a baby, and they'd moved into a women's shelter. But Rachel was much too young to remember. As far as she knew, the man who had raised her was her dad. So, it was a shock to discover that in a literal, biological sense, he wasn't.

Our own experiences with human fathers have a profound effect on how we respond to the Bible's claim that God is our Father. If you were well-loved and cared for by your father, you likely find it easy to relate to God in that way. If you were disappointed, abandoned, or abused by your earthly father, you may have a really hard time with the idea that God is your heavenly Father. But in the Gospels, we see Jesus calling God His Father and inviting us to call God our Father as well. This is a vital way in which the Bible invites us to relate to God. And it's a metaphor.

You might be thinking, *Wait! How can you say that calling God our Father is a metaphor? Isn't God truly our Father?* The answer is yes! God is more truly our Father than any human father could be. He is the perfect Father on whom human fatherhood is based. Just as we can use literal language to speak the truth or to lie, we can use metaphorical language to speak the truth or to lie. For example, I could make the claim that my father is a pilot. It would be a literal claim, but it would also be untrue. My dad's a strategy consultant! But if I tell you that God is my Father, I'm using a metaphor to communicate one of the truest things I could ever say about myself.

Today, we're going to spend time exploring how Jesus makes the powerful and life-changing claim that God truly is our Father. But we're also going to see that the distinction between literal and metaphorical claims is not always clear-cut.

READ LUKE 1:26-33. According to verses 31-32, whose son would Jesus be?

In just these two verses, Jesus is presented as the son of Mary, the Son of the Most High, and the son of David. Jesus is the literal, biological son of Mary, His mother. He is not the literal son of King David—who died centuries earlier—but He descended from David and He's heir to David's throne. What about the claim that Jesus is the "Son of the Most High"? Well, in Jesus's day, "Son of God" was a title for God's Messiah—His long-promised King. It would not have been taken in a literal sense. But as Gabriel's conversation with Mary unfolds, we discover that Jesus is also in a more literal sense the Son of God: He has no human father.

READ LUKE 1:34-35. What question did Mary ask Gabriel?

How does Gabriel's explanation point to Jesus as the Son of God in a literal sense?

The idea that Jesus was the Son of God in a more literal sense—that He did not have a human father, but that the Spirit of God made His mother pregnant—would have been completely shocking to first-century Jews. The Greek and Roman so-called gods were believed at times to impregnate human women and spawn demigods of various kinds. But the God of the Bible was completely different from these pagan deities. The God of the Bible is the one true God, the Creator of all things. He is a spiritual being, not embodied like we are. And yet the angel's message is that Mary's son will also be God's Son: no demigod, but fully God and fully man.

Why does it matter that Jesus is not the biological son of Mary's soon-to-be husband, Joseph, but rather the Son of God in a more literal sense?

In Jesus, we see the one person ever to have existed who is both fully human and fully God. His miraculous conception points us to this unfathomable reality. We see Jesus's Sonship affirmed at His baptism; when the heavens were torn open, the Spirit descended on Jesus like a dove, and a voice from heaven said, "You are my beloved Son; with you I am well-pleased" (Mark 1:11). Jesus is the Son of God. But amazingly, Jesus also invites us into that Father-Son relationship.

READ MATTHEW 6:5-14. In verse 6, to whom did Jesus say we should pray and why?

In verse 8, why did Jesus say we shouldn't babble like the Gentiles when we pray?

How does God's knowledge of our needs relate to the idea of God as our Father?

Famously, the Lord's Prayer begins with "Our Father" (v. 9). Does your own experience of human fatherhood make it easier or harder for you to see God as your loving, heavenly Father who knows your needs even before you make them known? Explain.

How does your experience more broadly impact how you relate to God as Father?

We might think that Jesus looked at human fathers and thought, *Huh, the best human fathers love their kids a bit like God loves me, so I'm going to use that metaphor to help folks understand that love.* But actually, it's no coincidence. If we understand the Bible as a whole, we'll realize that God the Father's love for God the Son existed before human beings ever did. God made human fatherhood in the first place not just to propagate the species, but so that the best of human fathers could be tiny signposts to His fatherly love!

READ JOHN 1:1-18. What do we discover about the relationship between the Word and God in verse 1?

What do we discover about the Word at the beginning of verse 14?

How does the second half of verse 14 reveal a Father-Son relationship within God Himself?

How does verse 18 connect back to verse 1 in describing the One who became flesh in the person of Jesus?

If your head is exploding right now, join the club! There's no way you and I will ever understand the Trinity. The nature of God Himself is utterly beyond our comprehension. But God has built relationships into our human experience that can give us little windows into the love between the members of the Trinity and into His love for us. One of those windows is fatherhood.

You may have had a wonderful experience with your own father, whose love for you felt like a reflection of God's love. Or you may have experienced a human father whose treatment of you was utterly unlike God's fatherly love. Perhaps you are a father and the love you feel for your kids may be giving you a little glimpse of God's incredible love for you. Or you may be a mother and getting a glimpse of God's love from a slightly different angle. While God is never called *mother* in the Bible (and we are never told to call Him that), the Bible does compare God to a mother. For example, in one of my favorite moments in Isaiah, God said to His people,

> Can a woman forget her nursing child, or lack compassion for the child of her womb? Even if these forget, yet I will not forget you.

ISAIAH 49:15

Moses rebuked God's people with an even more vivid maternal metaphor:

> You ignored the Rock who gave you birth; you forgot the God who gave birth to you.

DEUTERONOMY 32:18

As we give or receive maternal love, we also get a glimpse of God's tender, sacrificial, life-giving love for us. But Jesus especially invites us to call God our Father and to enter into the Father-Son relationship He has enjoyed from all eternity.

We've covered a lot of ground today, but don't be discouraged! We've seen how important metaphors can be in the Gospels and how Jesus's primary way of talking about God is at heart metaphorical. But we've also seen the complexity that can be woven into biblical metaphors and how the difference between literal truth and metaphorical truth is not always completely clear-cut.

I'm sitting across from my friend Rachel right now and I just asked her, "What's your dad's name?" She answered, "Bob." He's not her biological father. But he's more truly her father than the man whose genes helped make her body.

Whoever your biological father is, your most true Father is in heaven. Take a minute now to pray the prayer that Jesus taught His followers to pray:

> Our Father in heaven, your name be honored as holy. Your kingdom come. Your will be done on earth as it is in heaven. Give us today our daily bread. And forgive us our debts, as we also have forgiven our debtors. And do not bring us into temptation, but deliver us from the evil one.

MATTHEW 6:9b-13

DAY 2

THE GROOM

Three of my best friends and I have just arranged to watch a new Netflix®
adaptation of Jane Austen's *Persuasion*. The book is probably my favorite novel of
all time and a beautiful BBC adaptation of it is one of my favorite films. But from
what we can tell, this latest *Persuasion* movie will be dreadful. We plan to watch it
for the pleasure of complaining about how bad it is! If you're not familiar with the
story, Austen's novel centers on a quiet heroine, Anne Elliot, who had once been
engaged to a young lieutenant in the navy named Frederick Wentworth. Anne
broke off the engagement on the advice of an older friend but has never since met
any man to compare with her first love. Like Austen's other novels, *Persuasion* ends
happily, with Anne and Captain Wentworth finally marrying. But for most of the
book, we walk with Anne through loneliness and loss.

I don't know what your "relationship status" is right now. Single. Married.
Divorced. Widowed. Whichever category you fall into on that drop-down
menu, you might have a whole range of feelings about marriage. Maybe it's
something you long for. Maybe it's something you bitterly regret. Maybe
you're mostly happily married, but if you could go back and have a chat with
your single self, you'd try to talk some of your expectations about marriage
down a bit. Maybe you're contentedly single and enjoying the freedom and
opportunities for ministry that singleness brings. Maybe you're recovering from
a broken relationship, which you hoped would end in marriage, or maybe you're
recovering from a broken marriage.

In our study today, we're going to look at one of the most powerful metaphors in
the Bible. It's powerful because it speaks to our deep need for faithful and exclusive
love. And if we understand what God is saying to us through this metaphor, it will
transform how we think about human romance, because just as the best human
father could only ever be a pale imitation of our true Father in heaven, so the best
human husband could only ever be a fading copy of our true groom.

READ MATTHEW 9:14-15. What did Jesus mean by His response to
the question John's disciples asked Him?

Who are the guests, and who is the groom? What did Jesus say is going to happen to the groom?

Matthew, Mark, and Luke each feature this conversation (see Mark 2:18-20 and Luke 5:33-35). As so often is the case, John's Gospel takes a different approach but shines a light on Jesus the groom, nonetheless.

READ JOHN 3:22-30. What did John's disciples report about Jesus, and why was it troubling to them?

How did John respond to the report? Do you think his response was different from what his disciples might have expected? Explain.

How did John differentiate himself from Jesus? What did he say was his role, and what was Jesus's?

How did John say you can identify the groom in verse 29? How did the report about the people's actions point to Jesus as the groom?

How was John the Baptist's humility on display in these closing verses?

John made it clear to his disciples that they were not to be alarmed about what was happening. He reminded them of his role. He was not the Messiah or Christ, the great King that God had been promising for centuries to send, but rather, he was paving the way for Him. John was not the groom, but the groom's friend, and very happy to be in that place.

This metaphor of Jesus as the bridegroom doesn't come from out of the blue. Just as God's prophets had been promising for centuries that God would send His Messiah to His people, so they had also been casting God's people as a bride.

READ ISAIAH 54:5-8. How is God described in this passage?

How did God describe His people (v. 6)?

What is the past and future of their relationship (vv. 7-8)?

We see the same metaphor of God's marriage to His people in other prophets. For example, Ezekiel 16:1-32 begins with Jerusalem pictured as an abandoned newborn for whom God cared. Then, when she was fully grown, she was taken as His wife. But following that, Jerusalem started acting like a prostitute, giving herself to other so-called gods. She even sacrificed her children to them, as some of the pagan gods demanded. This idolatry of God's people was a spiritual equivalent to committing adultery against Him. Likewise, in Jeremiah, the Lord recalled the early days of His marriage to His people: "I remember the devotion of your youth, how as a bride you loved me and followed me through the wilderness" (Jer. 2:2, NIV). However, He continued, "But you have lived as a prostitute with many lovers—would you now return to me?" (Jer. 3:1b, NIV), and concludes, "'like a woman unfaithful to her husband, so you, Israel, have been unfaithful to me,' declares the LORD" (Jer. 3:20, NIV).

How well would you say this marriage between God and His people was going, according to the prophets?

What was the fundamental problem in their marriage?

Sin had rotted the foundation of the marriage between God and His people. They followed other so-called gods, and evil of all kinds sprang from this spiritual adultery. They didn't just need an extra date night or a marriage retreat. God's people needed a heart transplant—some way to deal once and for all with their ongoing sin.

When Jesus said He is the Groom, and when John the Baptist recognized Him as the true Husband of God's people, we see Jesus inhabiting God's role and bringing hope of a fresh start. But from the first, Jesus hinted at what is ahead for the groom. Remember what He said in Matthew 9:15?

> Can the wedding guests be sad while the groom is with them? The time will come when the groom will be taken away from them, and then they will fast.

Jesus's love for His people is the deeper reality human marriage is designed to echo. Explaining what Christian marriage should look like, the apostle Paul wrote: "Husbands, love your wives, just as Christ loved the church and gave himself for her" (Eph. 5:25). Quoting from Genesis 2, when God made the first man and woman and joined them together as "one flesh" (v. 24) in marriage, Paul explained that human marriage was created by God to be a signpost to the greater marriage between Jesus and His people:

> In the same way, husbands are to love their wives as their own bodies. He who loves his wife loves himself. For no one ever hates his own flesh but provides and cares for it, just as Christ does for the church, since we are members of his body. For this reason a man will leave his father and mother and be joined to his wife, and the two will become one flesh. This mystery is profound, but I am talking about Christ and the church.

EPHESIANS 5:28-32

How does our thinking on human marriage change when we realize that at its very best, it's pointing to Jesus's love for us?

Both inside and outside the church, people often talk as if marrying your "soulmate" is the ultimate human experience. If Jesus is our real Soulmate, how does this change how we think about lifelong singleness?

How does the reality that human marriage is modeled on Jesus's love for His people help us think about the clear boundaries the Bible puts around sexual relationships, confining sex to the specific design of male-female marriage?

How can the truth that Christian marriage is not a destination in itself but a signpost to the much greater reality of Jesus's love for us bring us comfort when we feel disappointed in human romantic relationships?

We may not feel today like we have the full experience of Jesus's husband-like love. Many of us (whether we're married or single) will still struggle with loneliness and longing, and we'll be tempted to look for our ultimate fulfillment in another mere human. But the Bible promises that one day we will experience our union with Jesus in its final form, and every longing of our hearts will be fulfilled.

READ REVELATION 19:6-8.

As we'll see tomorrow, "the Lamb" is one of Jesus's titles. One day we'll be filled with even more joy than John the Baptist was when he saw Jesus, as we'll all be included in the marriage of the Lamb.

Spend some time reflecting on that truth and bringing any pain and disappointment you feel in the area of human marriage to the Lord in prayer.

DAY 3

THE LAMB

After just celebrating Easter, we hosted some friends from our community group. I asked over lunch what Easter traditions they grew up with. Our friend Catherine, who's from Ghana, shared that when she was growing up, her family would buy a goat a few weeks before Easter. They'd fatten it up and then kill it and eat it on Easter day. If you, like me, were raised in a city in the West, you probably find two aspects of this family tradition jarring. First, while you were likely raised eating meat, you probably outsourced the slaughter of the animals. Second, while you may well be used to eating lamb, you're probably not used to eating goat. For no very good reason, goats and lambs occupy quite different places in western culture. Lambs are seen as cute and innocent and quite delicious. Goats have less positive vibes. We may eat goat's milk cheese, but we're unlikely to eat goat, and goats aren't our go-to animal for cuteness. And yet, in Ancient Near Eastern culture, lambs and goats would have been seen as very similar.

So far this week, we've looked at the metaphor of God as Father and of Jesus as Husband. We've seen how these metaphors were sketched out in the Old Testament Scriptures and then fleshed out in the New. The metaphor we're looking at today was also sketched out in the Old Testament, but rather than being built around a human relationship like fatherhood or marriage, this metaphor is built around an animal. As we saw at the end of yesterday's study, "the Lamb" is one of Jesus's titles in the New Testament. Today, we'll look at the roots of this metaphor, which can be traced all the way back to the beginning of God's chosen people.

> **READ JOHN 1:29-37.** How did John identify Jesus in this passage (vv. 29,34,36)?

So, Jesus is both the Lamb of God and the Son of God. We need to look back to the Old Testament to understand more of what this means.

In Genesis 12, God chose Abram to be the founding father of His people. It was hard to see how this would happen, since Abram and his wife Sarai were both old and had never been able to have kids. But in Genesis 15, God promised Abram that he would have a son, and through that son, God would give him as many descendants as the stars in the sky. In Genesis 17, when Abram was ninety-nine years old, God gave him a new name—Abraham—which means "father of a multitude." And then finally, in Genesis 21, the promised son was born. He was named Isaac, which means "he laughs." But in Genesis 22, God issued a heartbreaking command to Abraham.

READ GENESIS 22:1-14. What command did God give Abraham, and how did Abraham respond? How does verse 3 show that Abraham intended to obey?

In verses 7-8, what question did Isaac ask, and how did Abraham answer?

When Abraham received this shocking command, we can only imagine what was going through his mind. Even God's description of Isaac as "your son . . . your only son Isaac, whom you love," emphasized the deep affection Abraham had for Isaac (v. 2). And subsequent verses give us hints that their relationship was close. Despite that, it seems Abraham never hesitated to obey. He just gathered up the supplies and headed to Moriah with his son. Sometimes we picture Isaac in this story as a small boy. That's not likely the case. The word translated *boy* in verse 5 can also mean "young man," so we don't know how old Isaac was when this happened.[1] But a small child would not have been able to carry all the wood needed for the sacrifice (v. 6).

After Abraham made preparations for the sacrifice, he lifted his knife to kill Isaac, but the angel of the Lord stopped him. At that moment, Abraham looked up and saw a ram had been provided as a substitute for Isaac.

What did Abraham call the place?

How does this story help us to make sense of John the Baptist's claim that Jesus is the Lamb of God?

God spared Abraham's beloved son at the last minute. But He didn't spare His own beloved Son. Abraham's son asked, "Where is the lamb for the burnt offering?"(v. 7), and God provided an animal substitute sacrifice. But when John the Baptist looked at Jesus, he said, "Look, the Lamb of God, who takes away the sin of the world!" (John 1:29), and all four Gospels tell us the story of Jesus the Lamb being sacrificed for our sin.

When Abraham lifted the knife to sacrifice Isaac, the future of all God's people hung in the balance. Isaac was the one through whom God had promised He would generate a family as many as the stars in the sky. Isaac went on to father Jacob, whom God also called Israel, and Jacob's twelve sons became the starting points of the twelve tribes of Israel. One of Israel's sons, Joseph, was sold into slavery by his brothers and ended up in Egypt. But in God's sovereignty, this heartless decision was a key piece of God's redemptive plan. Joseph rose to power and was able to save his family and provide for them when they all ended up in Egypt. While there, God multiplied this family into a people group. But they ended up as slaves to the Egyptians, and God raised up a man named Moses to go and tell the Pharaoh of that day to let his people go. Each time Pharaoh refused, God sent a plague on Egypt. Before he sent the tenth and last judgment on Egypt, God told His people how they could be protected from it.

READ EXODUS 12:1-13. What were God's specific instructions in verses 3-7, and why was it so important that the people follow these instructions (vv. 12-13)?

The last plague was going to be devastating. But God made provision for His people. In English, we use different words for a young sheep and a young goat. And like we said earlier, most of us have very different feelings about the two. Hebrew has multiple words for sheep and goats—some of which could apply to either species—and goats were seen as just as delicious as lamb. The blood of either would be used that night to protect the people.[2]

The Exodus from Egypt had been celebrated at the Passover feast every year between when it happened and the day John the Baptist pointed at Jesus and said, "Look, the Lamb of God!" (John 1:29).

How does the Passover event help us understand what John the Baptist meant?

After God rescued His people out of Egypt, He called their leader, Moses, up on a mountain to receive His law. This law included instructions on how to build a tabernacle or "tent of meeting" where God's presence could be seen to dwell and where His people could make sacrifices to Him to atone for their sins. After that tabernacle was built, God gave Moses further instructions about those sacrifices. Many of those sacrifices called for lambs or young goats, including the sacrifice of a lamb at the entrance of the tabernacle every morning and evening (Ex. 29:38-43). Eventually, when God's people were established in their land, the portable tabernacle was replaced by the permanent temple. So, when John the Baptist pointed at Jesus and said, "Look, the Lamb of God!" the sacrificial system in the temple would have sprung up in the minds of his Jewish hearers.

Multiple physical lambs lie behind John the Baptist's metaphor of Jesus as the Lamb of God. But what about John's claim that Jesus is the Lamb of God who takes away the sin of the world? Hundreds of years before the prophet John the Baptist spoke these words, the prophet Isaiah foreshadowed this truth by comparing the mysterious Suffering Servant of the Lord to a lamb.

READ ISAIAH 53:1-8. By whom was this servant struck down (v. 4), what was the purpose of His suffering (v. 5-6), and how is the Suffering Servant like a lamb (v. 7)?

How does this passage help us understand Jesus as the Lamb of God who takes away the sin of the world?

Take time to reflect on Jesus as the sacrificial Lamb of God, who took our place and paid the price for our sin!

DAY 4

THE CUP

In *Harry Potter and the Half-Blood Prince*, Harry's headmaster and mentor Professor Dumbledore invites him to come on a mission. But he insists Harry follow one condition: "You must obey every command I give you without question. . . . Should I tell you to hide, you hide. Should I tell you to run, you run. Should I tell you to abandon me and save yourself, you must do so. Your word, Harry." And Harry responds, "My word."[3]

Harry and Dumbledore's mission is to recover a locket in which the evil Lord Voldemort has hidden part of his soul. But when they eventually find the locket, it's at the bottom of a liquid-filled bowl. Dumbledore realizes that the only way to get the locket out is to drink the liquid. Before he does so, he makes Harry promise to force him to keep drinking it, even if Dumbledore pleads with him to stop. So, Harry does. As Dumbledore experiences the agony of what turns out to be the magical drink of despair, Harry continues to make him drink until the bowl is drained. Dumbledore knows in advance what to expect from this drink. But he faces it nonetheless.

Today, we're going to get our heads around an Old Testament metaphor that Jesus reached for on the night He was betrayed. As with the metaphor of the "Lamb of God," if we don't understand the Old Testament background of this metaphor, we're not going to understand what Jesus meant when He pleaded with His Father to take "this cup" away from Him.

READ MATTHEW 26:36-46. On this night before His death, how was Jesus feeling, and what did He ask His closest friends to do for Him?

How did Jesus express His anguish to the Father with His body and His words (v. 39)?

Mark's Gospel gives us a snatch of Aramaic at this point:

> *Abba*, Father! All things are possible for you. Take this cup away from me. Nevertheless, not what I will, but what you will.

MARK 14:36

What were Jesus's disciples doing when He came back from praying (Matt. 26:40)?

Right before this passage, we heard Peter promising Jesus that even if he had to die with him, he would never deny him. What question did Jesus ask Peter in verse 40?

What did Jesus pray when He went back to pray alone a second time, and how many times did He pray this prayer?

If this passage was all the context we had for Jesus's prayer, we might think that He was just using drinking a cup as a metaphor for the physical death experienced on a cross. Crucifixion had been perfected by the Romans as an instrument not just of execution but also of torture. It was a long and agonizing death. Jesus was on the cross for six hours before he died, and the Roman governor Pilate was surprised He was already dead in that amount of time (Mark 15:44). You or I would certainly have pleaded with God to be spared from that horrific death. But if we dig into the Old Testament roots of this metaphor, we'll find that Jesus's dread went far beyond the physical torment of death on a Roman cross.

READ JEREMIAH 25:15-29. How did God describe the cup that Jeremiah was to take from His hand, and what was Jeremiah told to do with it?

What will happen to the nations that drink from the cup and why (v. 16)?

Why is it shocking that Jerusalem and the other cities of Judah are first on the list (v. 18) and are forced to drink the cup of God's wrath?

Summarize the message Jeremiah was to say to the nations in verses 27-29.

The cup of God's wrath is a vivid picture of judgment, and, like the metaphor of God's marriage to His people, it crops up in multiple prophetic texts (Isa. 51:17-23; Ezek. 23:28-34; Hab. 2:16). We even see this metaphor used in the psalms:

> There is a cup in the LORD's hand, full of wine blended with spices, and he pours from it. All the wicked of the earth will drink, draining it to the dregs.

PSALM 75:8

The cup of the LORD in these passages represents His judgment on nations. But Jesus, in the garden of Gethsemane, faced the prospect of drinking that cup of God's wrath against a whole world of sin all by Himself. That was why He pleaded, "My Father, if it is possible, let this cup pass from me. Yet not as I will, but as you will" (Matt. 26:39b).

This prayer of Jesus in Gethsemane and His prayer on the cross, "My God, my God, why have you abandoned me?" (Matt. 27:46b) might make us wonder if Jesus was really in on this plan. People sometimes portray Jesus as the victim of the Father's wrath against sin. But when Jesus died on the cross, He experienced not only the judgment of the Father but also His own judgment against sin.

READ REVELATION 6:15-17. Whose wrath are people trying to hide from in this depiction of the final judgment?

As we saw yesterday, the Lamb is the title for Jesus that's especially connected with His sacrificial death on the cross in our place. But here we see the Lamb not only as the Sacrifice but also as the righteous Judge of all the earth.

My guess is none of us enjoy thinking about the wrath of God against our sin. The metaphor of God as Father and of Jesus as Husband and Lamb of God who takes away the sin of the world likely brings us comfort. But the cup of God's wrath? Not so much. Most people have one of two reactions. Some are like my friend Andrei. Andrei became a Christian a couple of years ago after reading the Bible for himself for the first time. He found the wrath of God against his sin quite terrifying and spent some weeks dealing with that fear until it finally sank in for him that Jesus's death on the cross had truly taken that just punishment for him. He understood that Jesus drank the cup of wrath to the dregs so that anyone who puts their trust in Him won't have to. Others simply can't believe that God would be that angry at our sin. Isn't God supposed to be loving? Sure, we're not perfect, but the idea that God would really punish human sin feels so outside our natural ways of thinking.

But when we see Jesus reaching for the metaphor of the cup as He prayed to His Father, we see that it points both to the righteous anger of God against our sin and to His deep love for us. Like Dumbledore, who was ready to drink the magical drink of despair so that Lord Voldemort could be defeated, in the person of Jesus, God Himself was ready to drink the cup of His own wrath against a world of sin, so sin and death could be defeated, and so we could live eternally with Him. Jesus's human dread of this cup and pleading for another way to be found shows the true depth of the sacrifice He made, and God's refusal to take that cup away—His refusal to spare His Son, His only Son, Jesus, whom He loves—shows that the Father's love for us is just as deep as the Son's.

> Take some time to reflect on Jesus's willingness to drink the cup of wrath for you. What does this metaphor tell us about the seriousness of our sin and the depth of God's love?

DAY 5

THIS TEMPLE

My husband, Bryan, is currently building a house. Thank God he isn't doing all the construction work himself. He's done a lot of renovation projects in the past, and he's the kind of guy who really could just build a house from scratch— including all the electrical and plumbing work. But since he has another full-time job, he hired an actual contractor this time. He's also paid an architect to draw up the design. Before work on the house started a few months ago, Bryan showed me the architectural drawings. We imagined how the house would look from the lines on his screen. Now, the architect has sent us 3-D digital mock-ups of various rooms so we can get a better sense of what our home will look like. But most excitingly, as the new house is next door, we can look out of our window and see it being built.

In the book of Exodus, God gave Moses the architectural blueprints for a tabernacle where God could be worshiped. Later, the permanent structure of the temple was built according to God's architectural design. But when God sent judgment on His people in the form of the Babylonian invasion, the temple was destroyed, and they were exiled to Babylon. This was a catastrophic moment for God's people. But after several years, they were allowed to return to their land and rebuild the temple. By the time Jesus was born, this second temple had been renovated to become one of the most impressive buildings of that day. God's architectural design had become a magnificent building.

In our study today, we're going to look at Jesus's use of the temple as a metaphor, and we're going to see that the physical temple itself was in fact just an architectural design to point us to the real temple. To begin, we're going to look at the only story we have from Jesus's late childhood.

READ LUKE 2:41-50. How old was Jesus in this story, and how did He get separated from Mary and Joseph?

When Mary and Joseph found Jesus, where was He, and what was He doing?

How did Jesus respond when Mary challenged Him about His choice to stay behind, and what did He mean with the phrase "my Father's house" (v. 49)?

Jesus claimed the temple in Jerusalem as more truly His Father's house than Mary and Joseph's home in Nazareth. And when Jesus went back to the temple as an adult, He acted like He owned the place.

READ JOHN 2:13-22. When Jesus went to Jerusalem for the Passover, what did He find was happening in the temple?

How did He respond and why?

What did Jesus call the temple (v. 16)?

Jesus's disciples connected His actions with a moment in Psalm 69:

For I have endured insults because of you, and shame has covered my face. I have become a stranger to my brothers and a foreigner to my mother's sons because zeal for your house has consumed me, and the insults of those who insult you have fallen on me.

PSALM 69:7-9

By wreaking havoc in the temple, Jesus was expressing His deep desire that it should be a place of prayer and worship, not a profitable trading place for people who wanted to turn the need for sacrificial animals into a money-hungry enterprise. The "Jews" (probably those in charge of keeping order) wanted to know who Jesus thinks He is to be taking this kind of control in the temple.[4]

> What question did they ask Jesus, and how did He respond (John 2:18-19)?

The original temple, built by King Solomon, had been destroyed centuries earlier when God judged His people with foreign invasion. The initial rebuilding of the temple had been a painstaking business. Jesus's offer of a sign—"Destroy this temple, and I will raise it up in three days"—would have sounded both preposterous and sacrilegious to the Jewish leaders (v. 19).

> How did they misunderstand what Jesus said, and what did He really mean by that statement?

The forty-six years they referred to would have been the time taken for the extensive renovation of the temple building. But He wasn't talking about raising up a new building.

> According to verse 22, who understood what Jesus meant, and when did they finally get it?

Jesus was using a metaphor full knowing that His hearers wouldn't understand. Perhaps He also knew His words would be misquoted as evidence against Him at His trial. In Matthew 26:61 and Mark 14:58, we hear the accusation that Jesus said He would destroy the temple and rebuild it.

> So, how do you think this metaphor helps us understand who Jesus is?

The lesson is similar to what we discovered with the Lamb of God metaphor. The temple was designed to be the place where God was seen to dwell and where God's people could worship Him. In particular, it was the place of sacrifice and offering. But just as the lambs that were sacrificed at Passover or in the temple system were only pointers to Jesus—the real lamb of God, who takes away the sin of the world—so the temple itself was only a signpost to the real temple, which was Jesus's body. Jesus's metaphor is multi-layered. In addition to the connection with the temple being the place of sacrifice, the destruction of the first temple also held meaning. This event was a sign of God's judgment on His people for their sin. That judgment would fall again when the temple of Jesus's body was destroyed on the cross. But God would raise it up again at Jesus's resurrection from the dead, showing the return of God's presence with His people.

We also see the connection between Jesus's body and the temple symbolically enacted at the moment of Jesus's death.

READ MATTHEW 27:51; MARK 15:38; LUKE 23:45.

The curtain of the sanctuary was the barrier that separated off the most holy place in the temple, where God's presence was especially seen to dwell. This inner sanctuary was only entered once a year by the high priest. But at the moment Jesus died, the curtain was torn in two from top to bottom. Jesus's death broke through the barrier between God and His people and made the temple obsolete. The final sacrifice had been made, once and for all (Heb. 9:28). And after Jesus's death and resurrection, His disciples finally understood what His metaphor had meant.

As we close, take some time to reflect on the five metaphors we've explored this week: the Father, the Groom, the Lamb, the Cup, and the Temple.

How do these metaphors together help us understand who Jesus is?

How do they help us see that the Bible often communicates its deepest truths through metaphor?

UNDERSTANDING METAPHORS

IN THE GOSPELS ➤

Tips

➤ Metaphors compare one thing to another, but instead of saying "A is like B," they say "A is B."

➤ Speaking metaphorically is not lying, even though A is not literally B. Just as you can use literal language to speak the truth or to lie, you can use metaphorical language to speak the truth or to lie. For instance, I could say, "I have two sons and a daughter," and that would be a literal statement, but it would not be true. Or I could say, "My son is a tornado" and that would be a metaphorical statement, but anyone who knows my three-year-old would agree it is true!

➤ Metaphors are often used to communicate powerful, emotionally charged truths. For example, in Exodus 19:4 God said to His people, "You have seen what I did to the Egyptians and how I carried you on eagles' wings and brought you to myself." God didn't literally send eagles to carry His people out of Egypt, but His rescue of them at the Exodus was just as dramatic.

➤ Jesus frequently used metaphors—especially in John's Gospel, but also in Matthew, Mark, and Luke.

➤ Sometimes, it's obvious from the first that Jesus was using a metaphor: for example, when He said, "I am the vine, you are the branches" (John 15:5). Other times, Jesus's metaphors are intentionally hard to spot: for example, when He said to a Samaritan woman at a well, "If you knew the gift of God and who it is that asks you for a drink, you would have asked him and he would have given you living water" (John 4:10, NIV). We need to pay attention to the context to spot metaphors.

➤ When Jesus used metaphors, they tend to have deep Old Testament roots (like the metaphor of Israel as a vine or of God Himself as the source of living water). To grasp His meaning, we need to look at the Old Testament context.

Exercise

Listed below are Scripture passages where metaphors are used. Read the passages, identify the metaphors, and answer the questions to help understand the meaning.

READ MATTHEW 7:13-14. What metaphor do we see in this passage?

How does this passage show that recognizing a metaphor in a passage does not mean avoiding the hard truths we find in Scripture?

READ JOHN 10:11-18. What is the central metaphor in this passage, and how does this metaphor help us understand how Jesus relates to us?

READ PSALM 23:1-4. How does this Old Testament context help us understand more of Jesus's meaning in John 10?

READ ZECHARIAH 9:16; 10:3. How do these passages help us understand more of Jesus's role as the Good Shepherd?

Parables

If there is a human embodiment of the word *boisterous*, I think it might be my son, Luke. One of my daughters calls him "the human hurricane." If destruction is being wrought, Luke is likely to be found at the eye of the storm. But there is one surefire way to calm Luke down: read him a story. He might be in the middle of a full-scale, kicking, screaming tantrum, but if I open a book, he's suddenly quelled and quiet. Stories are powerful. And Jesus in the Gospels harnesses that power.

Just as metaphors are not intended to be taken literally but can communicate deep truths about God and us, parables are not intended to be read as historical narratives but rather as stories that communicate truth. Some are extensive, with multiple characters and stages of action. Those are the ones we'll focus on this week. But others are so brief they fit in a single verse. For instance, Matthew wrote, "He told them another parable: 'The kingdom of heaven is like leaven that a woman took and mixed into fifty pounds of flour until all of it was leavened'" (Matt. 13:33). Some are allegorical, with people or things in the parable representing other people or things: for example, a landowner representing God. Others tell a story in which a person (for example, a Pharisee or a tax collector) acts in a way that represents the larger group to which they belong—or overturns the expectations of how someone from that group would act.

Parables aren't stories about specific individuals; only one person in any of Jesus's parables has a name (Lazarus in Luke 16:19-31). Rather, they are stories with a meaning. Of course, many of the stories about actual historical events the Gospel authors told feature anonymous people and have meanings too. But it's important we understand the difference between a parable, which is deliberately fictional, and a Gospel narrative, which is telling us about something that actually happened—while also inviting us to understand a broader meaning.

There are a handful of parables in the Old Testament and one or two examples of parables attributed to rabbis who lived before Jesus.[1] But Jesus's use of parables is outstanding. Matthew, Mark, and Luke record dozens of parables of varying lengths— many of which focus on God's kingdom—while John's Gospel focuses instead on Jesus's metaphors.

This week, we'll look at five of Jesus's parables and hone our skills in understanding this kind of teaching. As with Jesus's metaphors, His parables often have Old Testament roots, and we will need to excavate those roots to understand what Jesus meant. And as with metaphors, we'll see that sometimes Jesus told a parable and expected His audience to understand, while other times, He told a parable and expected them not to understand.

SESSION *Four*

To access the video teaching sessions, use the instructions in the back of your Bible study book.

NOTES

Watch Rebecca's Session Four video.

Download the *Navigating Gospel Truth* leader guide at **lifeway.com/gospeltruth**

GROUP DISCUSSION GUIDE

What is a parable?

Why did Jesus use parables?

What is your favorite parable? Why?

Why is it important to understand how parables are used in the Gospels?

What part of the video teaching was most important for you?

DAY 1

THE SOWER

A few years ago, I met a woman in the checkout line at Target®. She'd recently moved to the United States from China. As we talked, I thought I'd shoot my shot and invite her to church. She came. Since English was not her first language, I also introduced her to a friend of mine who ran a Bible study specially designed for internationals. She started to attend. But when I asked her a few weeks later what she'd been learning at the Bible study, I was a little saddened by her answer. The previous week, they'd been studying Jesus's famous parable of the sower, and my Chinese friend said, "I think I'm the stony ground because sometimes I find the Bible hard to understand in English."

As we work through Jesus's parable of the sower today, we'll find that my friend misunderstood the story. None of Jesus's original hearers would have understood His teaching if He'd delivered it in English, and most Christians in the world today do not speak English as their native language. But we'll also find—surprisingly perhaps—that Jesus didn't just tell parables to make it easier for people to understand His teaching but also to make it harder: He wasn't trying to create a language barrier, like my friend was experiencing with the Bible in an English translation, but to create a spiritual barrier that people would need to push through to access His true meaning.

> **READ MATTHEW 13:1-9.** In this passage, Jesus used parables to teach a large crowd that had gathered by the seashore. Since Jesus's audience lived in an agrarian society, they would have quickly understood the context of the story.
>
> List the four soils and what happened to the seed that fell on each type of ground.

A tenfold harvest from the good soil would have been seen as a good crop. So a thirty, sixty, or hundredfold harvest would have been wild!

Whom did Jesus invite to listen to this teaching in verse 9?

This teaching is available to anyone who has ears: that is, pretty much everyone! In fact, Jesus called everyone to hear it. But Jesus didn't immediately explain what it meant.

READ MATTHEW 13:10-17.

After Jesus finished the story, the disciples asked Jesus why He was speaking to the crowd in parables. In Mark's account, it's clear this was the larger group of disciples who inquired, not just the twelve apostles (Mark 4:10).

How did Jesus answer, and what did He mean (Matt. 13:11)?

Jesus was differentiating here between the crowds who showed up for a short time to see healings or hear stories and His more persistent followers.

What surprising claim did Jesus make in verse 12, and how does this claim in the context of this conversation start to explain the parable of the sower?

How did Jesus describe the effect of the parables in verse 13?

To explain more, Jesus quoted from a stunning chapter in Isaiah.

READ ISAIAH 6:1-13. Summarize what happened in verses 1-8.

In Matthew 13:14-15, Jesus quoted Isaiah 6:9-10. How did Jesus apply the LORD's message in Isaiah to the people of His day?

How did Jesus contrast the crowds in general with His actual followers (see vv. 16-17)?

How does this quotation from Isaiah and its application not just explain why Jesus taught the parable of the sower but also start to explain what the parable means?

Jesus went on to explain the parable of the sower in detail, which was not His usual practice with parables. More typically, He would leave the audience to work out what the story meant, or He would provide a key to interpreting the message, but not give a step-by-step interpretation. However, here we see Jesus explaining multiple elements of the parable.

READ MATTHEW 13:18-23. According to verse 19, what does the seed represent?

List how Jesus interpreted the seed falling on the different soils.

What do we learn from this parable, and how do we apply it in our current context? What does it say about what we're to be doing in spreading the gospel and how it will be received?

How does this parable show the incredible fruitfulness of God's Word while also showing that different people can hear the exact same message and respond in different ways?

We are to spread the word of the gospel wherever we go, with the understanding that not everyone who hears the word will receive it. In fact, in the parable, only one kind of ground out of four received it. From the surface, that doesn't look very successful—not until you see the abundant harvest that comes from the one.

Even as I worked on this study, I found that the parable worked on my heart. Honestly, the parable of the sower has never really spoken to me much before. It doesn't have the emotional force of many other longer parables. But the more I spent time with it, the more I found it gripped me and made me want to sow God's Word freely and trust Him with the results. The harvest is so plentiful. When Matthew recorded Jesus going through all the towns and villages, teaching in synagogues, preaching the good news of the kingdom, and healing every disease and sickness, he wrote,

> When he saw the crowds, he felt compassion for them, because they were distressed and dejected, like sheep without a shepherd. Then he said to his disciples, "The harvest is abundant, but the workers are few. Therefore, pray to the Lord of the harvest to send out workers into his harvest."

MATTHEW 9:36-38

Take time now to pray that God would send more workers to His harvest field and ask Him to show you ways you could increasingly be part of that amazing gospel work!

THE PRODIGAL SON

The other day, my elder daughter, Miranda, asked me if I've ever been moved to tears just by reading a passage in the Bible. I couldn't think of a time that I had. I'm English, so I'm slow to cry! But just now, as I was reading today's parable, tears sprang to my eyes.

Last week, we saw how Jesus used the metaphor of God as Father to communicate a vital truth not only about His own relationship with His Father but also about the father-child relationship we can enjoy with God. This metaphor of God as Father is also embedded in some of Jesus's parables. Most movingly, we find it in the famous parable of the prodigal son.

At the beginning of the chapter, the Pharisees and scribes were grumbling that Jesus was eating with tax collectors and sinners. So, Jesus told them a parable in which a man who owned a hundred sheep left ninety-nine of them to find the one that was lost. Then, after he found the lost lamb, he called his friends and neighbors together to rejoice with him. Jesus concluded, "I tell you, in the same way, there will be more joy in heaven over one sinner who repents than over ninety-nine righteous people who don't need repentance" (Luke 15:7). Next, Jesus described a woman who had ten silver coins, lost one of them, and scoured her whole house until she found it. Then, she called her friends and neighbors together to rejoice with her. Again, Jesus concluded, "I tell you, in the same way, there is joy in the presence of God's angels over one sinner who repents" (Luke 15:10). Following these two stories, Jesus told a much more extended parable with a similar message.

READ LUKE 15:11-32. What do we find out about the heart of the father early in this story (v. 12)?

In verses 11-16, what selfish and reckless choices did the younger son make, and what position did it put him in?

According to Jewish law, pigs were unclean animals. So, this Jewish man hired himself out to a Gentile as a pig herder: a doubly shameful situation to be in that underlined his desperation. Not only was he working among the pigs but he was so hungry that he was willing to eat what the pigs were eating yet was unable to do so.

What happened in verse 17 that helped him further realize the foolishness of the choices he made up to this point? What was his plan (vv. 18-19)?

At this point in the story, we don't know if this son felt true remorse for what he'd done or if he was just experiencing the negative effects of his sin and working out an escape strategy. But he headed home in any case.

List all the details of the loving father's actions in verses 20-23. How do they communicate his eagerness to have his son back?

How did the father explain his actions to his servants in verse 24?

The father's actions were as wild as the son's but in the opposite direction. The son took his inheritance and hurtled headlong into sin until he hit rock bottom. The father welcomed the son back with what feels like disproportionate extravagance. There's no rebuke. No probation period. No, "Fine, let's start you off as a hired servant, and then we'll see how you behave." The father ran to his loser of a son, flung his arms around him, kissed him, dressed him in clothes that signified great honor, and threw a party to celebrate. Why? Because his son was dead and is alive again. He was lost and is found. Friend, if you have repented and believed in Jesus, this is how God feels about you! I don't know if your sin looked as dramatic as this younger son's. Rebellion against God can look a lot of different ways. It can look like this son. Or it can look like the chief priests and elders, who thought they held the moral high ground while they looked down on other "sinners." They even thought they could teach the Son of God Himself a moral lesson. But whatever our sin looks like, God's love looks like the love of this father. Extravagant. Outrageous. Tender. Undeserved.

But the story isn't over.

> How did the older son react when he heard about the party being thrown to celebrate his brother's return? How would you summarize his grievance in verses 29-30?

I'll be honest with you. This detail about the younger son using prostitutes sparked something in my heart as well. Prostitution was tragically pervasive in the ancient world. In the wider Greco-Roman world, it would not have even been seen as immoral, let alone exploitative, to sleep with prostitutes. But Jesus's lifting up of women and welcoming of prostitutes into God's eternal kingdom planted the seeds for the moral outrage you and I might feel today. There's a piece of me that thinks I'm morally superior to the younger son. But that's a very dangerous feeling to have. That's exactly how the older son felt. It's interesting Jesus left the ending of the story for that elder son ambiguous.

> How did the father respond to his firstborn son in verses 31-32?

> How does the older son resemble the Pharisees and scribes at the beginning of the chapter?

Like the scribes and Pharisees, the older son was still outside the party when the story ends. We don't know if he chose to enter in or not. If you, like me, relate closely to the older son, we need to watch ourselves.

> Spend some time praising God for His extravagant, unbreakable, fatherly love—a love that ran toward you in the person of His own Son Jesus, a love that grabs you in a warm embrace and wipes out every record of your sin. This is the Father's love for you and me.

DAY 3

THE PHARISEE AND THE TAX COLLECTOR

Confession: I don't do my taxes. Don't worry, I'm not an actual criminal. But I'm completely terrible at paperwork and probably would land myself in prison for some unintentional mistake if I attempted it! Thankfully, Bryan is extremely good at paperwork, so he takes care of it for both of us. Before you think we're just a stereotypical couple, Bryan is also much more interested in clothes and fashion and interior design than I will ever be—and he's better at cooking and cleaning. Basically, he's omnicompetent! But even he doesn't enjoy filing taxes.

For Jews of Jesus's time and place, tax-paying was doubly painful. First, most of them were poor, and paying taxes hurt them financially. But on top of this, the Jews of Jesus's day were paying taxes to their Roman overlords. This meant they were funding their oppressors, and for many Jews, it felt like a religious compromise since the Romans were pagans. But some Jews were doing very well from this whole scenario. The tax collectors were Jewish men who had chosen to conspire with the Romans to extort taxes from their own people. And worse, they also helped themselves to additional payments on top of the required tax to pad their own pockets. All this led to tax collectors being seen as moral scum. But more than once, Jesus sided with tax collectors over the most seemingly religious Jews. He even recruited a tax collector to be one of his twelve apostles!

When Jesus called His tax collector disciple, Levi—who was also known as Matthew—the Pharisees and scribes complained that Jesus was eating with tax collectors and sinners.

READ LUKE 5:27-32. What metaphor did Jesus use in response to the Pharisees' and scribes' complaint, and what did He mean by it?

Would the Pharisees and scribes have seen themselves as spiritually healthy or sick? How would their self-diagnosis have impacted their response to Jesus?

It's clear to the reader here that Jesus was siding with the tax collectors, the ones who knew they needed Him, against the Pharisees and scribes who didn't think they did. But it may not have been clear to the Pharisees. Later in Luke, Jesus told a parable in which He explicitly sided with a tax collector against a Pharisee.

READ LUKE 18:9-14. How did Luke describe the people Jesus addressed with this parable (v. 9)?

A tax collector and a Pharisee went to the temple to pray. As the Pharisee stood to pray, what did he thank God for (v. 11)?

The tax collector might well have fallen into all the sinful categories the Pharisee mentioned: greedy, unrighteous, adulterous. The Pharisee wasn't wrong about the tax collector's sin.

What examples of his own righteousness did the Pharisee list in verse 12?

1.

2.

By fasting twice a week, this Pharisee was going above and beyond what the Old Testament law required (see Lev. 16:29-31; 23:27-32; Num. 29:7). And giving a tenth of *everything* he got was also going beyond what the law required (see Deut. 14:22–23). The Pharisees were known for their commitment to the law. This man was a shining example of religious observance. So, the second half of Jesus's story comes as a shock.

How does Jesus's physical description of the tax collector in Luke 18:13 signal a contrast with the Pharisee?

The fact that the tax collector was "standing far off" may mean he was standing in the court of the Gentiles (v. 13). Minimally, he didn't consider himself worthy to occupy the same space where the Pharisee had set himself up. The fact that he "kept striking his chest" communicates mourning and repentance (v. 13). This man really knew he was spiritually sick.

What was the tax collector's simple prayer?

What outcome did Jesus say each man received as a result of his prayer (v. 14)?

If you think about it, each man got what he asked for. The Pharisee asked for nothing and got nothing. The tax collector asked for mercy and received it. The one thing the Pharisee and the tax collector have in common is they both believed the tax collector was a really dreadful sinner. But as so often happens in the Gospels, the Pharisee could only diagnose sin in other people. He could not see it in himself, and so he didn't ask for mercy.

How is the twist in this parable similar to the twist in the prodigal son story?

Unlike seed falling on the different kinds of ground in the parable of the sower, the Pharisee and the tax collector in this story aren't standing in for something else. But they are representatives of the groups to which they belong. The Pharisee isn't every Pharisee, and the tax collector isn't every tax collector. But they're also not just individuals who happen to be a Pharisee and a tax collector respectively. This isn't a story about two particular men. It's a parable about two different types of people.

Matthew recorded a confrontation Jesus had with the chief priests and elders in which Jesus told a mini parable that draws together strands from the prodigal son and the parable of the Pharisee and the tax collector. Jesus was in the temple, and the religious leaders had been challenging His authority. He responded by asking them whether they thought John the Baptist's baptism had come from heaven or from men. Not wanting to get crossways with the watching crowd, who believed John the Baptist was a prophet, the chief priests and elders said they didn't know. So, Jesus said He also wouldn't tell them by what authority He was acting. Instead, He told a parable.

READ MATTHEW 21:28-32. Summarize the parable.

What offensive claim did Jesus make in verse 31, and what did He mean?

This teaching would have been utterly offensive to His hearers. Jesus was saying that the most notorious sinners of their day—the tax collectors and the prostitutes—were entering God's kingdom ahead of the top religious leaders. Why? Because the "sinners" were repenting of their sin and believing in Jesus while those who were meant to be shepherding God's people were rejecting Him.

Take some time to reflect on how offensive this claim is, even today. We may not think of tax collectors as the apex sinners in our culture, but reflect on how shocking it is that God welcomes even the most sinful people who will turn and trust in Him while seemingly "good people" who think they don't need Jesus cannot come into His kingdom.

DAY 4
THE VINEYARD OWNER

As we alluded to on Day One, many of Jesus's original hearers would have been farmers eking out a living from the land. Thus, many of Jesus's parables draw agricultural analogies—like the parable of the sower (Matt. 13:1-23), the parable of the wheat and the weeds (Matt. 13:24-30), and the parable of the mustard seed (Matt. 13:31-32). Often, these agricultural parables are shorter and have less of a developed plot. But today, we'll explore a longer agricultural story known as the parable of the vineyard owner.

In one of Jesus's famous "I am" statements in John's Gospel, Jesus presented Himself as a vine: "I am the true vine, and my Father is the gardener. Every branch in me that does not produce fruit he removes, and he prunes every branch that produces fruit so that it will produce more fruit" (John 15:1-2). By using this metaphor, Jesus was not only pointing His hearers to a plant and farming practice with which they would have been familiar, but He was also pointing them to an Old Testament metaphor in which God was pictured as a farmer and His people as a vineyard.

Our parable today follows directly from the parable of the two sons with which we ended our study yesterday. In that parable, the two sons were sent to work in their father's vineyard. The first Jewish hearers may have made the connection with the metaphor of Israel as God's vineyard. In our parable today, the Old Testament connection is unmistakable. At multiple points in the Old Testament, God's people are compared to a vine or a vineyard. For example, in Jeremiah, God asked, "I planted you, a choice vine from the very best seed. How then could you turn into a degenerate, foreign vine?" (Jer. 2:21) Later, God lamented, "Many shepherds have destroyed my vineyard; they have trampled my plot of land. They have turned my desirable plot into a desolate wasteland" (Jer. 12:10). But the most important Old Testament context for the parable we'll explore today comes from the prophet Isaiah.

READ ISAIAH 5:1-7. Isaiah described how "the one I love" planted a vineyard on a fertile hill. What did the vineyard owner do to maximize the chances of a good harvest? Did he get what he expected? Explain.

In verse 3, the narrative voice shifts to first person for the rest of the passage as the vineyard owner asks the residents of Jerusalem and men of Judah to adjudicate between him and his vineyard.

What two questions did he pose, and what actions was he going to take?

Isaiah explained the meaning of the story in verse 7. Summarize what he said.

God had planted the nation of Israel. He had loved and cared for His people, expecting a harvest of justice and righteousness. Instead, they produced injustice and despair.

With this story fresh in your mind, turn back to Matthew 21. As a reminder of the context, Jesus was in the temple in Jerusalem and addressing the chief priests and elders (vv. 23-25). He had just told the parable of the two sons and made the following highly offensive claim to the religious leaders: "Truly I tell you, tax collectors and prostitutes are entering the kingdom of God before you" (v. 31). Then, He dealt another blow.

READ MATTHEW 21:33-46. Summarize the parable (vv. 33-39).

Thinking back over the history of God's people before Jesus came, whom do you think the servants in this parable sent by God to His vineyard might represent?

Jesus didn't explain this parable, but He definitely applied it. He asked them how the owner of the vineyard would deal with the tenant farmers. Their response was quick and decisive, "He will completely destroy those terrible men . . ." (v. 41).

How does this response show that Jesus's parable was working to draw His audience in?

It seems they were completely engrossed in the story and didn't realize they had pronounced their own judgment. Then, Jesus shamed these chief priests and elders, the theological experts of their day, by asking them, "Have you never read in the Scriptures . . . ?" (v. 42).

Jesus's quotation comes from Psalm 118. Here it is in context:

Open the gates of righteousness for me; I will enter through them and give thanks to the LORD. This is the LORD's gate; the righteous will enter through it. I will give thanks to you because you have answered me and have become my salvation. The stone that the builders rejected has become the cornerstone. This came from the LORD; it is wondrous in our sight. This is the day the LORD has made; let's rejoice and be glad in it.

PSALM 118:19-24

Why did Jesus quote this psalm? Who was He saying are the builders, and who is the stone?

READ ISAIAH 8:13-15. How does this passage connect with Jesus's statement in Matthew 21:44 and help us understand the identity of the stone?

How does Jesus explain His parable to the chief priests and elders in verse 43?

How did the chief priests and the Pharisees respond to Jesus's parable and application?

What did Jesus communicate about His own identity in the parable of the vineyard owner and its explanation?

What does Jesus's parable communicate about the patience and justice of God?

The vineyard owner showed incredible patience with the tenants. Rather than coming after them when they assaulted and murdered the first servants he sent, the vineyard owner gave his tenants a second and third chance, even sending his own son. But this does not mean that he would not ultimately judge them. Such it is with God. His patience is great, but His justice is true.

Spend some time reflecting on God's patience and His justice. How have you seen His patience in your own life? How are you tempted to presume on God's patience, rather than to recognize the seriousness of your sin and your deep need for Jesus's death in your place?

DAY 5
THE WEDDING BANQUET

Bryan and I got married twice. In June 2007, we got married in England. Then, in October, we got married in Oklahoma so that more of his family and friends could attend. I again wore the wedding dress my grandma had made me, and the pastor Bryan had always thought would officiate at his wedding remarried us. It was fun! But one of the things we discovered while planning two weddings on two continents was that the wedding customs in our cultures were significantly different. In British culture, weddings happen in the late morning or afternoon, not in the evening. The groom wears a "morning suit" complete with a top hat, not a tuxedo. Bridesmaids are what Americans call "flower girls." Adult women at British weddings wear hats or—minimally—elaborate hair decorations called *fascinators*. (If that word means nothing to you, Google it!) But one of the biggest differences between my expectations and Bryan's when it came to weddings was the guest list. Bryan's family hosted weddings in a large church hall with an open buffet, a space big enough to invite all their friends and family. So, as our UK wedding drew near, Bryan kept remembering people he wanted to invite, and I realized his mental guest list included everyone he knew!

We saw last week that John the Baptist called Jesus the *groom*, as did Jesus Himself. This connected with the Old Testament metaphor of God as a faithful, loving Husband to His all-too-unfaithful people. The parable we'll look at today focuses on the guest list for the wedding of a king's son. It follows directly after the parable of the vineyard owner. But while Jesus didn't explain the vineyard owner parable's meaning until the end, He gave an interpretive prompt for this parable at the beginning.

READ MATTHEW 22:1-10. What did Jesus say the kingdom of heaven is like in verse 2?

How did the people on the guest list treat the king's invitations and those who delivered them?

How does this situation remind you of the parable of the vineyard owner?

How did the king respond to those who refused to come, and what was his reasoning (vv. 7-8)?

How did the king expand the invitation, and who ended up coming (vv. 9-10)?

How does this line up with Jesus's claim in Matthew 21:31 that the tax collectors and prostitutes were getting into the kingdom of God ahead of the religious leaders?

The second round of invitations in Jesus's parable has two dimensions. One is relatively obvious to us: God is inviting all the moral riffraff, including tax collectors and prostitutes, into His kingdom. The other is less clear, but we get a clue to it from another time Jesus described the kingdom of heaven as a banquet. In Matthew 8, a Roman centurion whose servant was terribly sick approached Jesus. Jesus offered to come and heal him, but the centurion replied, "Lord, . . . I am not worthy to have you come under my roof. But just say the word, and my servant will be healed" (Matt. 8:8).

This Gentile soldier recognized Jesus's complete authority, and Jesus was amazed by his faith. He said to His followers:

> Truly I tell you, I have not found anyone in Israel with so great a faith. I tell you that many will come from east and west to share the banquet with Abraham, Isaac, and Jacob in the kingdom of heaven. But the sons of the kingdom will be thrown into the outer darkness where there will be weeping and gnashing of teeth.

MATTHEW 8:10b-12

Here, we see Gentiles entering God's kingdom and enjoying the banquet while some of the Jewish "sons of the kingdom" rejected Jesus and were thrown out—not because they weren't invited but because they didn't come.

Let's go back to Matthew 22 and read the similarly troubling end of Jesus's parable.

READ MATTHEW 22:11-14. What did the king notice in verse 11?

What did the king ask the guest, and how did the guest respond (v. 12)?

What did the king do in response to this (v. 13)?

What do you think is the meaning of this part of the parable? How is this a warning to all of us?

What final interpretation of His parable did Jesus give in verse 14?

The man who was not dressed for the wedding gives us a picture of someone who seemingly responds to Jesus's invitation and comes along with God's people but is not truly converted. In Matthew 7, Jesus warned His disciples against false prophets and said they will be known by their fruit. He went on to say,

> Not everyone who says to me, "Lord, Lord," will enter the kingdom of heaven, but only the one who does the will of my Father in heaven. On that day many will say to me, "Lord, Lord, didn't we prophesy in your name, drive out demons in your name, and do many miracles in your name?" Then I will announce to them, "I never knew you. Depart from me, you lawbreakers!"

──────────

MATTHEW 7:21-23

Take some time now to reflect on your own heart. Tragically, it's possible to grow up in the church but not be a true follower of Jesus. So, how can we know if we are true followers or if we'll end up like the man who came to the wedding feast but wasn't dressed for it? The parable of the Pharisee and the tax collector can help us. So can the parable of the prodigal son. If you feel keenly aware of your own sin and your unworthiness to be included in Jesus's kingdom, that's a good sign. If being known as a Christian is generally a status boost to you in your community, it's worth asking yourself some hard questions.

As we've looked at some of Jesus's parables this week, we've seen He tells stories that get to the heart of both the extravagance of God's love and the seriousness of His judgment. We've seen how parables communicate indirectly, sneaking up on us and springing a trap on our self-righteousness. Parables are meant to be pondered and taken to heart. Pick the parable that spoke to you most this week and spend some time reflecting on its message.

How has this week helped you better understand Jesus's use of parables in the Gospels?

Which of the parables we talked about this week spoke to you the most? Why?

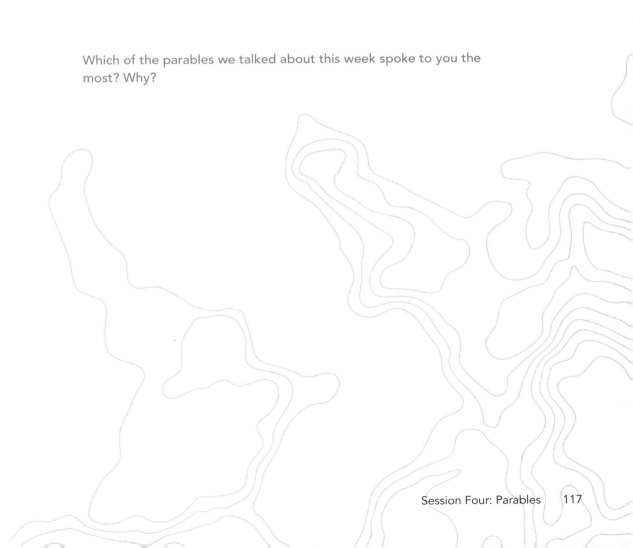

UNDERSTANDING PARABLES

IN THE GOSPELS ❯

Tips

❯ Parables are fictional stories with a true meaning.

❯ Parables can be long and complex or short and simple, but in either case, they are designed to make us think.

❯ In Matthew and Luke in particular, Jesus often taught in parables.

❯ Jesus's parables ranged in length and form. Different kinds of parables include:

- Single point comparison: parables designed to draw out a single point of comparison and should not be pressed beyond that.

- Multiple point allegories: parables in which multiple people or things in the story correspond to multiple people or things in real life.

- Example stories: parables where the characters in the story represent people from that same group in real life.

- "How much more?" stories: parables where Jesus was both comparing and contrasting someone in the story with God.

❯ Parables are a form of indirect communication. Sometimes, they're straightforward from the first. Other times, they spring a trap on the hearer who is drawn in before realizing the parable has been told against her. We're meant to ponder parables!

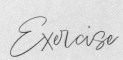

Listed below are references for three parables in the Gospels. Read each one, title it, and summarize it. Then, determine the kind of parable it is: single-point comparison, multiple-point allegory, example story, or "How much more?" story. Finish by journaling the meaning of the parable and how it might apply to you.

	MATT. 13:47-50	MATT. 18:21-35	LUKE 12:13-21
TITLE			
SUMMARIZE			
KIND			
MEANING AND APPLICATION			

Teaching

When my best friend, Rachel, was first exploring Christianity, she was embarrassed to find herself attracted to Jesus. She'd grown up in a non-religious home and had previously identified as an atheist. She thought Christians were stupid to believe what they did. What's more, when she was fifteen, she'd fallen in love with a senior girl at her high school and had gone on to date that girl. But when Rachel was a freshman at Yale, her girlfriend broke up with her. Rachel was devastated. In the midst of her emotional crisis, she began to wonder if maybe there was a God after all. Not knowing what to do, she started googling® religious terms and found herself stumbling on Jesus. She knew Christians were opposed to same-sex sexuality, so she really didn't want to be drawn to Jesus. But the more she read of the Gospels, the more intrigued she became. One of the things she found most attractive about Jesus was His extreme intelligence. Whenever He was challenged by His opponents, He would decimate them with His wit. When He was asked a question, He always seemed to have the perfect answer. She still thought Christians were stupid, but she was beginning to see that Jesus wasn't stupid at all.

In the last two sessions, we looked at Jesus's use of metaphor and parables to sift His audience, forge Old Testament connections, spring traps, and lodge His teaching in our minds. This week, we'll look at some of the other forms of teaching Jesus used to grab His hearers' attention and make them really think. In particular, we're going to look at Jesus's use of hyperbole, commandment, blessing, contradiction, and aphorism.

If some of these words mean nothing to you yet, don't worry! By the end of the week, you'll know what they all mean. But you won't be feeling clever and superior. If you've listened to what Jesus is saying, you'll likely be thinking something not unlike what Rachel thought: *Wow, we Christians can be really stupid. But Jesus is incredibly smart.*

SESSION *Five*

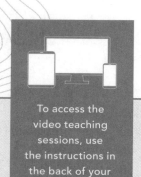

To access the video teaching sessions, use the instructions in the back of your Bible study book.

NOTES

Watch Rebecca's Session Five video.

Download the *Navigating Gospel Truth* leader guide at **lifeway.com/gospeltruth**

GROUP DISCUSSION GUIDE

What is hyperbole, and how did Jesus use it in the Gospels?

Jesus was accused of loosening the law and commandments, but in reality, He tightened them. In what way?

What is an aphorism, and did you use one today? If so, what was it? How did Jesus use them in His teaching?

Why is it important to understand how hyperbole, commandment, blessing, contradiction, and aphorism are used in the Gospels?

What part of the video teaching was most important for you?

HYPERBOLE

"Mum is going to kill me."

My daughter, Miranda, was telling me just now about a task she'd forgotten to do at school—a task I'd reminded her about this morning. She confessed it slipped her mind. When I asked her about it a few minutes ago, she recalled the moment she realized she'd forgotten: *Mum is going to kill me*, she had thought. I said, "Don't worry. I'm never actually going to kill you. Well, if I ever do, it will be a total accident and I'll be heartbroken afterwards." We laughed.

Miranda knows I love her with my whole heart, and I'm never going to literally kill her. But when she makes that statement, she's using something called hyperbole, which means extreme exaggeration that's not meant to be taken at face value. We use it in everyday speech (at least, my kids do), and we see it in songs and stories. For instance, my all-time favorite singer, Ella Fitzgerald, sang a song titled, "Cry Me A River" in which she demands that her former beloved cry a river over her because that's what she's done over him.

In 2002, Justin Timberlake came out with a hit with the same name. We all know no one has ever cried an actual river. But we get the point. A song titled "Cry a lot for many days, weeks, or even years" would not have had the same success!

Today, we're going to look at Jesus's use of hyperbole. We'll see how hyperbole works to give powerful emphasis to Jesus's points and to make His audience really think. We'll also hone our skills at spotting and understanding this particular rhetorical device.

READ MATTHEW 23:23-24. Where in these verses was Jesus using hyperbole?

How did you spot it?

According to the Old Testament law, both gnats and camels would have been considered unclean and not allowable to eat. It's pretty easy to avoid eating a camel, but you might eat a gnat by accident, so people would sometimes filter their wine to make sure no gnats were in it. So Jesus was saying that the scribes and Pharisees being very careful on the small things, like tithing their herb gardens, while failing in the much more important matters of justice, mercy, and faithfulness, was like putting great effort into straining out tiny bugs while swallowing whole camels.

Imagine if Jesus hadn't used hyperbole but had just left it at verse 23. What difference would it have made to understanding this section of teaching, and how would it have affected how memorable and striking it is?

What would it look like in our lives to be straining out gnats and swallowing camels when it comes to the desperately important matters of justice, mercy, and faithfulness?

READ MATTHEW 7:1-5. Where do you see hyperbole in these verses?

Imagine the visual of a man with a two-by-four stuck in his eye trying to pick a splinter out of someone else's! It's comical and absurd—like swallowing a camel!

What point was Jesus making with this hyperbolic image?

This is one of Jesus's most memorable teachings, mainly because of the power of this hyperbole. It grabs our attention. It forces us to think about what He's saying and how it applies to us when we look down on others and think that we have the right to judge them because our sin is so much less than theirs. But interestingly, Jesus's point here isn't that we should never challenge a brother or sister on his or her sin.

LOOK BACK AT VERSE 5. What things did Jesus tell us to do, and what did He mean?

READ LUKE 14:25-27. What shocking claim did Jesus make in verse 26?

We know from Jesus's teachings elsewhere in the Gospels that He specifically condemned people who make religious excuses for not honoring and caring for their parents (Mark 7:8-13). He also takes marriage so seriously as a one-flesh union made by God Himself that even His disciples were taken aback (Matt. 19:1-10) and that He put a high value on children (Matt. 19:13-15). So, we know that Jesus wasn't calling us to literally hate our families. What, then, did He mean? Jesus was highlighting the closest family ties a human being could have—parents, spouses, children, siblings—and saying that His followers' love for everyone else should seem like hatred in comparison to their devotion to following Him.

Well-meaning Christian parents sometimes say, "Of course, I need to put my family first." But actually, if that is really what we're doing, it's idolatry. Jesus must come first. We must be ready to leave everyone and everything for Him. He's calling us to nothing less than worship. But if we truly do love Jesus first, our love for Him will flow out into love for those around us as we seek to obey His command to love one another sacrificially as He has loved us (John 15:12). Ironically, by loving Jesus first, we'll end up loving others more, not less.

What second shocking claim did Jesus make in Luke 14:27?

People on their way to be crucified were often expected to carry the wood of their own cross. Jesus used this distressing visual to picture what it means to follow Him. Jesus Himself was going to be crucified quite literally, but that was not what He was literally intending for all of His followers.

How do we know Jesus was not expecting the crowd to take Him literally when He made this statement?

It's tempting to recognize a statement like this as hyperbole and therefore fail to feel its force. Take a minute now to meditate on Jesus's statement here.

Knowing that the cross's only purpose was an instrument of death, how does that help us understand the meaning of what Jesus said?

How are you giving up your life for Christ, and in what ways are you taking a hit for following Him?

Are you willing to face shame and ridicule for your faith? Explain.

Are there things you really wish you had that you're not buying so that you can give more to gospel work and those in need?

Are there sins you're deeply tempted toward that you're saying no to and feeling the pain of that self-denial?

Those questions are all searching ones for me as I sit with this teaching. God does not call us to seek persecution or hardship out for its own sake. But the more we are living faithful, fully-committed, Jesus-centered lives, the more we can expect to face opposition and hardship. If we're settled into a comfortable Christian life, it may be a whole lot less Christian that we realize. Pray with me now for the Lord's help to take up your cross and follow Him!

COMMANDMENT

After God rescued His people from slavery in Egypt, He gave them instructions on how they should live. These instructions are known as the law, and they include the famous "Ten Commandments." The term "the law" can be a bit confusing. Sometimes it refers to the laws God gave His people and sometimes to the first five books of the Bible—also known as the Torah—in which this law is recorded. A story is told of a famous Jewish rabbi named Hillel, who lived in the first century BC. A Gentile came to him and said he would convert to Judaism if Hillel would teach him the entire Torah while he was standing on one leg. Hillel accepted the challenge and replied, "What is hateful to you, do not do to your neighbor. That is the whole Torah; the rest is the explanation of this—go and study it!"[1]

Jesus was asked a somewhat similar question—not by a Gentile but by an expert in the law. The Old Testament contained hundreds of commandments, but there were certain scenarios in which two commandments could be in conflict with each other. In a case like that, you needed to know which one should win out. We encounter similar situations even today. For example, in one of my favorite scenes in *The Sound of Music*, the Nazi's cars won't start, so they're unable to pursue the von Trapp family. Two of the nuns have stolen vital parts of their cars. Since stealing is forbidden in the Scriptures, each nun confesses to the head nun, "Reverend mother, I have sinned."[2] But it was clearly right for them to steal in this instance.

READ MATTHEW 22:34-40. What did Jesus say was the greatest commandment (vv. 37-38)?

Jesus quoted from Deuteronomy 6:5, which was one of the best-known commandments in the Jewish law. It was part of the *Shema*—a prayer recited daily by faithful Jews. Living in a world that worshiped many pagan gods, the Jews believed in only one God—the God who made the heavens and the earth and had called them as His people. Loving this one God, Jesus affirmed, is the most important commandment of all. But Jesus, quoting Leviticus 19:18, emphasized a second commandment.

What was the second commandment, and how did Jesus describe it?

How is the second commandment "like" the first?

What did Jesus say about these two commandments together (Matt. 22:40)?

Both the first and the second commandments call us to love. According to Jesus, love of God and love of others is the driving force behind the whole Old Testament law. As we've already seen in this study, Jesus in the Gospels often argued against the people of His day who were known for taking God's law very seriously. But we totally misunderstand Jesus if we think He didn't care about God's law. In fact, He made it crystal clear He does. In His famous "Sermon on the Mount," Jesus faced this misunderstanding head-on.

READ MATTHEW 5:17-20. How does what Jesus said about "the Law" and "the Prophets" (v. 17) in this passage indicate how seriously He takes the Old Testament law?

What challenging claim did Jesus make in verse 20?

Jesus's hearers would have considered the scribes and Pharisees as the absolute experts at keeping the law. The idea that you'd have to have more righteousness than them to get into God's kingdom would have sounded absolutely crushing. But Jesus challenged them further.

READ MATTHEW 5:21-22. "Do not murder" was the sixth of the famous Ten Commandments. How did Jesus make this law more stringent in verse 22?

I don't know about you, but I've never committed murder. Just reading the Ten Commandments, I could feel quite good about myself on number six. But have I ever been angry with a brother or sister? That's a whole other matter.

READ MATTHEW 5:27-28. How did Jesus make the seventh commandment more rigorous?

Once again, if I was just reading the Ten Commandments, I would feel OK about the adultery one since I've never been in an adulterous relationship. But according to Jesus, if we've even played out sexual scenes in our minds with someone we're not married to, we've committed adultery in our hearts.

And Jesus was not done.

READ MATTHEW 5:29-30. What radical instruction did Jesus give?

Did He mean for us to take this action literally? If not, what was His point?

There's one sense in which Jesus's teaching here is hyperbole. He was recommending radical action. If you find something in your life that is pulling you toward sin, cut it out. Maybe you're accessing pornography on your phone. Much better to throw it in the river than to let it be a gateway into sin. Maybe you're finding that social media is stoking your envy or anger or self-righteousness. Much better to delete your account than to let that be a gateway into sin. Maybe you have wealthy friends who pull you toward spending money on luxury items you really don't need and away from sacrificial giving to the poor. Step back from those friendships. These could all be good applications of Jesus's teaching here. But there's another sense in which Jesus's teaching isn't hyperbole. It literally would be better to lose an eye or a hand than to be thrown into hell. So, why aren't there more deliberately blind Christians? The more we understand Jesus's teaching, the more we'll realize our problems go much deeper than our eyes or our hands. The problem is with our hearts.

In Mark 7, Jesus was confronted by the scribes and Pharisees because His disciples weren't ceremonially washing their hands before they ate in the way prescribed by the tradition of the elders—a set of regulations developed by earlier rabbis, which went beyond the Old Testament law. Jesus called them hypocrites and quoted Isaiah 29:13 against them, "This people honors me with their lips, but their heart is far from me" (Mark 7:6, ESV). Later, Jesus explained what really makes a person clean or unclean, and it's not what you eat or how you eat it but what comes out of your heart: "For from within, out of people's hearts, come evil thoughts, sexual immoralities, thefts, murders, adulteries, greed, evil actions, deceit, self-indulgence, envy, slander, pride, and foolishness" (vv. 21-22).

Losing an eye or a hand would be terrible. But Jesus identified the source of our sin as our deepest self: our heart. We can't cut that out. And that's the point. As we read Jesus's teaching on the law, we find that we haven't the smallest hope of meeting His standards. We don't just need a little self-improvement. We need Jesus's fulfillment of the law and His death in our place. If we let this truth lodge in our hearts, we'll see how our obedience must spring from it.

READ JOHN 15:12-17. What commandment did Jesus give His disciples in verse 12, and what example of love did He use to clarify the meaning?

How did Jesus qualify and explain His friendship with His followers in verses 14-15?

How does this passage, especially verse 16, show that Jesus takes the initiative in His relationship with us, not vice versa?

We don't earn Jesus's love by our obedience to His commands. If we could, we wouldn't have needed Him to save us. But Jesus's love for us—expressed most powerfully in His death in our place—prompts our attempts at obedience. We can never achieve perfect righteousness ourselves. But we can attempt (however clumsily) to trace the footsteps of the One who did.

DAY 3

BLESSING

What does it mean to be *blessed*?

In Genesis 1, we see God blessing the first humans: "God blessed them, and God said to them, 'Be fruitful, multiply, fill the earth, and subdue it'" (Gen.1:28). In Genesis 9:1, God blessed Noah and his sons in similar terms. Then, in Genesis 12, God promised Abraham: "I will bless those who bless you, I will curse anyone who treats you with contempt, and all the peoples on earth will be blessed through you" (v. 3). In the Old Testament, we often see God blessing His people in visible ways: family, prosperity, peace.

Today, we see the language of blessing all around, not least on social media. Perfect pictures of happy families with the simple comment #blessed. Mugs. Wall hangings. I even saw a tire cover yesterday with the three words: *Thankful. Grateful. Blessed.* We associate the word *blessing* with relational and material prosperity—the enviable lifestyle. But Jesus's take on blessing would be an out-and-out commercial failure.

Jesus had a massive audience. Great crowds were following Him, from Galilee and Decapolis in the north, as well as from Jerusalem and Judea in the south, and from beyond the Jordan in the east. Jesus was on prime time. So, what did He do? He preached His Sermon on the Mount and began with nine surprising blessings, sometimes called the Beatitudes. (This title comes from the Latin term *beatitudo* which means "blessedness.")[3]

READ MATTHEW 5:2-12. Fill in this table with the situation and the blessing for each of the nine Beatitudes.

BLESSED ONES	BLESSING
Poor in spirit	Kingdom of heaven

The Greco-Roman world in which the Jews of Jesus's day were living was very much a might-is-right world. The strong dominated the weak, and this was celebrated. Winners were winners. But not in Jesus's economy.

How would you summarize the differences between Jesus's view of who is blessed and our culture's view?

What was Jesus trying to help His followers understand with this teaching?

How have you seen these beatitudes being played out in your life?

Which of these beatitudes really speaks to you and why?

How do verses 10-12 especially cut against our expectations of what it means to be #blessed?

We tend to think that being persecuted, even in the milder ways we might encounter it in the West—such as being accused of being hateful by colleagues or not getting a job for holding to Christian sexual ethics—is a sign that things are wrong in our society. But according to Jesus's teaching here, in one sense, being persecuted is a sign that things are right in the church. Presently, I'm going back-and-forth on email regarding one of my kids who is experiencing the cost of being a Christian at middle school today. She's being slandered by a friend who is making her out to be hateful when she's not. It's painful, but it shows that she's OK with not fitting in if that's the price for following Jesus.

If we're never out-of-step with our non-Christian peers to the point they speak evil against us, that's probably when we should worry. But we must also make sure that when we face opposition, it's on account of Jesus and we've been acting in the ways He described in this passage: being poor in spirit, meek, merciful, peacemaking, and so forth, and not being harsh, self-righteous, and judgmental.

When any experience of opposition or persecution does come, we must also remember Jesus's shocking commandment later in the Sermon on the Mount.

You have heard that it was said, Love your neighbor and hate your enemy. But I tell you, love your enemies and pray for those who persecute you, so that you may be children of your Father in heaven.

MATTHEW 5:43-45a

Luke's Gospel records a shorter summary of what's recorded in the Sermon on the Mount in Matthew. Luke's account also begins with blessings, but Luke focused on four blessings and paired them with four woes.

READ LUKE 6:20-26.

Luke's four blessings mirror blessings number one, four, two, and nine from Matthew. We don't need to worry about the differences between Matthew and Luke's accounts here. We know each of the Gospel authors made his own selection from Jesus's many teachings. But we're going to look at the differences in Matthew and Luke's blessings to see if we can spot overall themes.

Spend a minute noting the differences between the blessings listed in Luke and the ones listed in Matthew.

LUKE	MATTHEW	DIFFERENCES
Blessed are you who are poor, because the kingdom of God is yours.	Blessed are the poor in spirit, for the kingdom of heaven is theirs.	
Blessed are you who are hungry now, because you will be filled.	Blessed are those who hunger and thirst for righteousness, for they will be filled.	

LUKE	MATTHEW	DIFFERENCES
Blessed are you who weep now, because you will laugh.	Blessed are those who mourn, for they will be comforted.	
Blessed are you when people hate you, when they exclude you, insult you, and slander your name as evil because of the Son of Man. Rejoice in that day and leap for joy. Take note—your reward is great in heaven, for this is the way their ancestors used to treat the prophets.	You are blessed when they insult you and persecute you and falsely say every kind of evil against you because of me. Be glad and rejoice, because your reward is great in heaven. For that is how they persecuted the prophets who were before you.	

What difference did you notice in terms of whom Jesus was talking about in Matthew and Luke?

How was Luke's focus different from Matthew's in his first and second blessing?

We tend not to see poverty as a sign of God's blessing. We don't post on social media, "I lost my job today. #blessed." Or "Look at the food stamps I'm using to feed my family! #blessed." More likely, we'd post a photo of the new house we bought or the gourmet meal we're enjoying. If instead of buying a house, we're facing eviction because we can't afford the rent, we might start wondering if God is really with us. But Jesus's first and second blessings in Luke turn this mentality on its head. He reinforced this thinking when He listed Jesus's four woes to pair with the four blessings.

> **READ LUKE 6:24-26.** When you think about God's blessing in your life, do you automatically connect it with material and relational prosperity? Explain.

How does Jesus's teaching on God's blessing challenge what we hear about blessing even from some social media accounts or radio shows that claim to be Christian?

If you trace the theme of blessing through the Gospels, you'll find that those who are blessed are not the materially successful or well thought of but the ones who are obeying God. They may feel the cost of that obedience now, but ultimately, they will feel God's blessing. In His famous parable of the sheep and the goats, Jesus talked about the final judgment day when He will say to those who have shown obedience to Him by caring for the poor, sick, and imprisoned, "Come, you who are blessed by my Father; inherit the kingdom prepared for you from the foundation of the world" (Matt. 25:34b). Let's live like citizens of Jesus's kingdom now, whatever the cost!

DAY 4

CONTRADICTION

I hate the way you talk to me
And the way you cut your hair.
I hate the way you drive my car
I hate it when you stare.
I hate your big dumb combat boots
And the way you read my mind.
I hate you so much it makes me sick,
It even makes me rhyme.
I hate the way you're always right,
I hate it when you lie
I hate it when you make me laugh,
Even worse when you make me cry.
I hate it when you're not around,
And the fact that you didn't call.
But mostly I hate the way I don't hate you,
Not even close, not even a little bit, not even at all.[4]

If you don't recognize this poem, you must have missed the classic 1990s film *10 Things I Hate About You*! Loosely based on Shakespeare's play *The Taming of the Shrew*, the film follows the love stories of two sisters. The younger sister, Bianca, isn't allowed to date until her antisocial older sister, Kat, has a boyfriend. So, a guy who wants to date Bianca pays a guy named Patrick to get him to persuade Kat to date him. Of course, by the end of the film, Kat has fallen in love with Patrick. She writes a poem listing all the things she hates about him and reads it to their class. But rather than being a hate poem, it's really a love poem.

Maybe a friend has asked you, "Isn't the Bible full of contradictions?" It's a common question.

In our study on narrative, we looked at some of the seeming contradictions between the different Gospels and how they don't actually discredit the Gospels.

Today, we're going to look at seeming contradictions within Jesus's teaching and discover that rather than discrediting Jesus's skill as a teacher, these contradictions actually display His skill.

READ MATTHEW 16:24-25. What seems to be the contradiction in this passage?

If we understand the word *life* in exactly the same sense both times, Jesus's second statement in verse 25 seemingly contradicts the first one. But this is intentional on Jesus's part. He was expertly pushing us to think about what life we value more: life here and now or life with Him forever.

New Testament scholar, Peter Williams, points out that we frequently find contradictions along these lines in John's Gospel in particular.[5]

READ JOHN 7:25-29. What reason did the people of Jerusalem give for thinking Jesus was not the Christ? Did Jesus agree with them?

READ JOHN 7:40-44. In verses 41-42, what reason did people give for thinking that Jesus was not the Christ?

When people ask me where I'm from, I usually say "London" because that's where I mostly grew up. But I was actually born in a small town in England called Windsor. Likewise, Jesus was born in Bethlehem, the City of David, and was raised in Nazareth in Galilee, but that's not where He ultimately came from.

READ JOHN 8:12-14. So Jesus told His audience they didn't know where He came from. Do you think Jesus was talking about His birthplace, hometown, or something else? Explain.

How was it possible for people to know where Jesus came from (7:28), yet not know where He came from (8:14)?

READ JOHN 8:19. In 7:28, Jesus said, "You know me and you know where I am from." But in this passage, He told them they didn't know Him. How is it possible for people to know Jesus and not know Him?

READ JOHN 14:1-9.

Here, Jesus's audience was different from His audience in John 7 and 8—He was talking only to His disciples. But we see Jesus exploring different senses in which people can know and not know Him and where He's going.

How did Thomas misunderstand Jesus's claim in verse 4?

How did Jesus respond to Thomas?

An alternative translation of verse 7 would be, "If you had known me, you would have known my Father also. From now on you do know him and have seen him" (ESV).

The disciples had been living with Jesus for years at this point. What could He have meant by saying, "If you had known me"—as if they didn't know Him?

How does this theme of them knowing/not knowing Jesus continue in verses 8-9?

It's very possible to know Jesus in one sense and not know Him in another. Even Jesus's closest disciples didn't really get who Jesus was until after His death and resurrection. It's possible to know where He came from in human terms but not to know where He came from in spiritual terms. John's Gospel pushes us to probe different meanings of multiple words as we explore who Jesus is. We see John's use of contradictions from the very first.

READ JOHN 1:1-18. What seeming contradiction do we see in verse 1?

How does this paradox of the Word both being with God and being God help us to understand who Jesus is?

What possible contradiction do we find in verses 11-12?

How can it be true that Jesus's own people—the Jews—did not receive Him, but that all of Jesus's apostles and virtually all of His first disciples were Jews?

Why do you think John didn't just say, "While many of the Jews of Jesus's day did not receive him, some did"?

READ JOHN 14:8-9 AGAIN. How does what John said in 1:18 contradict what Jesus says in 14:9?

How does this tension help us understand what John said in the second half of John 1:18?

It's sometimes hard for us to sit in tension. We tend to resolve all tension and make things simple. But Jesus doesn't offer us an easy ride. All four Gospels reveal a Jesus who is both human and divine. What's more, they present us with a man who insists that there is only one true God, who calls God Father, but who also claims through both His words and actions that He is God. There is a paradox at the heart of the Christian understanding of who God is. We're never going to crack that nut. But in multiple passages, the Gospel authors invite us to press into this paradox and other seeming contradictions as we grapple with who Jesus is.

Spend some time now reflecting on what it means to know Jesus and how it might be possible to know Him in a limited sense but not really know Him at all.

APHORISM

"It takes a village to raise a child."

This line has become so well-known that it often gets applied to contexts outside parenting. Receiving an Oscar, someone might just say, "I want to thank all the incredible people who made this film possible. It takes a village." A short, pithy observation that captures a truth like this is called an aphorism, and if you think about it, you probably hear them every day. "No pain, no gain." "It's ten percent inspiration and ninety percent perspiration." "The early bird catches the worm." "If it ain't broke, don't fix it." Or, my personal favorite, "Done is better than perfect."

The point of an aphorism is not to teach an unbreakable truth. You actually can raise a child without a village. And sometimes, I've been an early bird and caught no worms at all! But aphorisms aim to communicate wisdom. Don't be consistently late to the scene and expect to get first dibs. Don't think that raising a child is best done without a broader community.

Jesus often used aphorisms in His teaching, sometimes as the punch line of a parable or other longer teaching form. New Testament scholar Richard Bauckham writes this:

Compared with the narrative parables, the short aphorisms of Jesus, of which there are many more, generally receive less attention. Readers with modern reading habits tend to skim quickly through them, whereas they are meant to be paused on and pondered.[6]

Like His parables and metaphors, Jesus's aphorisms are designed to burrow their way into our minds and make us really think.

READ MATTHEW 7:7-12. What three related claims did Jesus make in verse 7, and how did He double down on these claims in verse 8?

Did Jesus intend these to be universal claims: that is, anyone who asks anyone for anything will get it? Explain.

How do verses 9-11 help us understand the relationship that Jesus has in mind between the one asking and the one receiving?

How does Jesus's punch line in verse 11 help us understand why we might sometimes ask God for something and not receive it?

Does this knowledge that God might sometimes lovingly withhold the things we ask for mean we shouldn't do as Jesus says in verse 7 and ask, seek, and knock?

Bauckham explains that Jesus would not have delivered each aphorism once, but rather used them multiple times in His teaching, and that some of Jesus's aphorisms are "deliberately riddling and meant to be puzzled over."[7]

READ MARK 4:25. What curious claim did Jesus make in this verse?

READ MATTHEW 13:10-12, WHICH FOLLOWS FROM JESUS'S PARABLE OF THE SOWER. How does Jesus's aphorism in verse 12 echo His aphorism in Mark 4:25 and help us to understand it better?

READ MATTHEW 25:14-30. Note verse 29 where Jesus used the same aphorism. How does the parable of the talents help us understand more of what Jesus means by this aphorism?

How does Jesus's repeated use of the same aphorism in different contexts and with slightly different words even within one Gospel help us understand the differences we see between Jesus's recorded teachings in one Gospel versus another?

One context in which Jesus used aphorisms was in dialogue with His opponents.

READ MATTHEW 22:15-22. What aphorism did Jesus use in this passage?

How did He use it to strategically answer His opponents?

The question the Pharisees posed was a trap. They knew if Jesus said they should pay taxes, then He would be endorsing their pagan, Roman overlords. But if He said they shouldn't, they could report Him to the Romans for stirring up rebellion. So, He answered them with the aphorism "Give, then, to Caesar the things that are Caesar's, and to God the things that are God's" (v. 21). It summarized in a pithy and memorable form how people should relate to Caesar and to God. When understood from a Jewish point of view, the meaning goes deep. In the very first chapter of the Hebrew Scriptures, God made human beings "in his own image" (Gen. 1: 27). If the denarius coin belonged to Caesar because it bore the emperor's image, Jesus's hearers themselves belong to God because they bear His image. The Pharisees were amazed at His answer and left speechless.

One other way Jesus used an aphorism was right after quoting a proverb.

READ LUKE 4:16-30. Summarize the situation in verses 16-22.

What proverb did Jesus expect them to quote and why (v. 23)?

What aphorism did Jesus deliver in verse 24?

Do you think Jesus literally meant that no prophet is accepted in his hometown? Explain.

How does the people's response prove the truth of Jesus's aphorism?

Pick one of the aphorisms we've explored today that struck you in particular. Write it below and give your reason for choosing this one.

Spend some time thinking and praying about that truth and asking Jesus to shape your life this week with His words.

UNDERSTANDING TEACHING
IN THE GOSPELS ➤

Tips

Jesus used an incredible range of tools in His teaching. In this session of study, we were able to identify and explore five different ways Jesus taught the truth. Here's a reminder of each style:

Hyperbole: Extreme exaggeration to make a powerful point
Example: Matthew 23:24: "You strain out a gnat, but gulp down a camel!"

Commandment: Teaching calling for direct obedience, often channeling or interpreting the Old Testament law
Example: Matthew 5:38-39: "You have heard that it was said, An eye for an eye and a tooth for a tooth. But I tell you, don't resist an evildoer. On the contrary, if anyone slaps you on your right cheek, turn the other to him also."

Blessing: An expression of God's favor on a group or individual, often used by Jesus to show how different God's priorities are to ours
Example: Matthew 5:4: "Blessed are those who mourn, for they will be comforted."

Contradiction: Two seemingly contradictory statements that stand in tension with each other and make us puzzle over the different senses in which a word might be used
Example: Matthew 16:25: "For whoever wants to save his life will lose it, but whoever loses his life because of me will find it."

Aphorisms: Short, pithy sayings designed to be memorable and provocative
Example: Mark 10:31: "But many who are first will be last, and the last first."

Exercise

Listed below are several references in the Gospels that feature one of the forms of teaching highlighted in this session's personal study. Read each passage and then determine whether it is hyperbole, a commandment, a blessing, a contradiction, or an aphorism.

READ JOHN 8:15-16. "You judge by human standards. I judge no one. And if I do judge, my judgment is true, because it is not I alone who judge, but I and the Father who sent me."

Form of Teaching:

READ LUKE 5:31. "Jesus replied to them, 'It is not those who are healthy who need a doctor, but those who are sick.'"

Form of Teaching:

READ MATTHEW 11:28-30. "Come to me, all of you who are weary and burdened, and I will give you rest. Take up my yoke and learn from me, because I am lowly and humble in heart, and you will find rest for your souls. For my yoke is easy and my burden is light."

Form of Teaching:

READ MATTHEW 18:21-22. "Then Peter approached him and asked, 'Lord, how many times must I forgive my brother or sister who sins against me? As many as seven times?' 'I tell you, not as many as seven,' Jesus replied, 'but seventy times seven.'"

Form of Teaching:

READ JOHN 20:29. "Jesus said, 'Because you have seen me, you have believed. Blessed are those who have not seen and yet believe.'"

Form of Teaching:

Dialogue

When I was a kid, my dad read to me Sir Arthur Conan Doyle's classic series about Sherlock Holmes. Holmes is a gentleman detective with extraordinary powers of deduction. The stories are written from the perspective of Holmes's roommate and companion, Doctor Watson, who has Holmes's permission within the fictional world to write up their adventures. Holmes is almost always ten times cleverer than anyone else in the story—including Watson. So in the course of the narrative, Watson asks the questions we as readers would have asked. This helps us to see Holmes's process, either as it unfolds or in the aftermath when he and Watson are discussing the case. The meaning comes out in the dialogue.

As we've already seen in our study so far, the Gospel authors often recorded Jesus in dialogue with His disciples and with His opponents. We've seen Him in public confrontations with the Pharisees and scribes and in private conversations with His followers. In our studies this week, we're going to focus on individual dialogue as a specific form of communication in the Gospels. We'll see that Jesus didn't just deliver disembodied truths into a vacuum. He taught real people. This is especially true in John's Gospel, where we get to listen in on some deep conversations with fleshed-out individuals.

In some ways, dialogue in John's Gospel plays a parallel role to parables in Matthew, Mark, and Luke. Jesus's teaching is embedded in a story. Just as Jesus's parables often posed a challenge to the hearers—making them lean in to understand, or springing a trap to catch them unawares—Jesus's dialogues often involved a push-and-pull with His interlocutor. He would issue a challenge, and they often failed (at least at first) to comprehend. But as the conversation progressed, the meaning emerged. We learn from both Jesus's challenge and His dialogue partner's response.

To access the video teaching sessions, use the instructions in the back of your Bible study book.

SESSION Six

NOTES

Watch Rebecca's Session Six video.

Download the *Navigating Gospel Truth* leader guide at **lifeway.com/gospeltruth**

GROUP DISCUSSION GUIDE

When you think of a conversation Jesus had with someone in the Gospels, which one comes to mind? Why?

How did that dialogue forge connection, frame action, feature tension, and force reaction?

When you think of those conversations, what do you learn about Jesus's heart, character, and purpose?

Why is it important we recognize and study the conversations Jesus had with people in the Gospels?

What part of the video teaching was most important for you?

DAY 1

NICODEMUS THE PHARISEE

If you and I sat down and played a Gospels word association game, I could pretty much guarantee a few of your answers, even if you're relatively new to reading the Bible. If I said, "Judas," you'd likely say "traitor." If I said, "Samaritan" you'd probably respond, "Good!" And if I said "Pharisee," you'd have some kind of negative response—most likely "hypocrite." But most Jews of Jesus's day would have had quite different reactions to those last two words. "Samaritan" would have made them think "bad" and "Pharisee" would most likely have made them think "good."

Among the different Jewish religious groups of Jesus's time and place, the Pharisees were the most influential. They specialized in applying the Old Testament law to everyday life. In addition to adhering to the Old Testament law itself, they followed oral traditions passed down from earlier Pharisaic rabbis: for example, extra regulations concerning ritual washing. The Pharisees thought the best response to the reality that God's people were living under pagan, Roman overlords was to show resistance by maximizing their own holiness and purity.

Today, the Pharisees are most famous for their confrontations with Jesus. Time and again in the Gospels, Jesus was criticized by the Pharisees because He broke their rules. And time and again, Jesus criticized the Pharisees for their hypocritical living. So, it is especially striking that the first encounter Jesus had with a Pharisee in John's Gospel was not a hostile encounter at all.

READ JOHN 3:1-15. What do we find out about Nicodemus in these first few verses?

The fact that Nicodemus was "a ruler of the Jews" (v. 1) indicates he was part of the Sanhedrin: the Jewish ruling council made up of around seventy priests, scribes, and lay elders. The note that he came at night might indicate his hesitancy to be seen with Jesus, but it also could be an editorial comment by John on the condition of his heart. Early in his Gospel, John made a clear distinction between darkness and light, and more than once used "night" or "dark" to indicate spiritual condition.[1] Also, it seems that Nicodemus comes, in some sense, as a representative of a larger group—"We know that you are a teacher . . ." (v. 2).

> What did Nicodemus say about Jesus, and what reason did he give for his statement?

> How did Jesus respond in verse 3?

In Matthew, Mark, and Luke, the kingdom of God/heaven is a massive theme. But in John's Gospel, that language only appears in this dialogue with Nicodemus. This helps us to see the connection between "the kingdom of God/heaven" in Matthew, Mark, and Luke and "eternal life," which is a key theme of Jesus's teaching in John.

At this moment in his dialogue with Nicodemus, Jesus issued a challenge. He told this senior Jewish leader that far from being an elder among God's people, he hadn't even been born yet! Here Jesus's language is deliberately enigmatic: in the original Greek, "born again" can also mean "born from above."[2]

> How did Nicodemus react to Jesus's curious claim, and why do you think he reacted in that way?

> How was Jesus's response in verse 5 similar and different to His first response in verse 3?

When Jesus used the phrase "born of water and the Spirit," He wasn't talking about two separate events (v. 5). He combined them to represent being born from above.[3]

FLIP BACK TO JOHN 1:32-34.

John the Baptist's testimony that Jesus would baptize with the Holy Spirit is our closest context in John's Gospel and helps us understand what Jesus meant here. Jesus is the only One through whom we can enter the kingdom of God.

Note that when Jesus said, "you must be born again" in John 3:7, He was using the plural form of "you." In England, where I come from, there's no way to say this. But in Oklahoma, where my husband is from, the plural of "you" is "y'all!" This also points to what we noted earlier from verse 2 that Nicodemus was here on behalf of a group. Now, Jesus was reflecting that plural back to him.

> What natural phenomenon did Jesus bring up in verse 8 to describe the work of the Spirit?

In Greek the same word—*pneuma*—can mean spirit or wind.[4] (English words like *pneumatic* and *pneumonia* come from this Greek word.) Likewise, in Hebrew, the same word—*ruach*—can have both meanings.[5]

> How does this double meaning help us to understand what Jesus was talking about in verse 8?

Jesus was saying that like the wind, which you can't see or know from where it originates but can only feel and see its effects, so it is with those who are born again. The spiritual change that takes place in them is a mystery, difficult to define. But the result of that work of the Spirit is seen in their lives.[6]

If you're still finding Jesus a bit hard to understand, Nicodemus did too. "How can these things be?" he asked in verse 9. Jesus responded with a question that confronted Nicodemus. He came to Jesus as "a teacher of Israel"—someone who should know about the things of God (v. 10). But Jesus exposed his ignorance.

Perhaps unsurprisingly, Nicodemus didn't speak again in this dialogue. But Jesus continued with a third statement introduced and emphasized with the phrase, "Truly, I tell you." Like Nicodemus in his opening statement, Jesus spoke in the plural: "we speak what we know and we testify to what we have seen, but you [plural] do not accept our testimony" (v. 11). Jesus moved back to singular for Himself but stayed with the plural for Nicodemus and the group he represented in verse 12 when Jesus questioned their ability to believe.

How did Jesus double down on the claim from Nicodemus (v. 2) that He had indeed come from God in verse 13?

"The Son of Man" was Jesus's favorite way of referring to Himself. We see Him use this enigmatic title in all four Gospels. This is the second time He used it in John's Gospel. The first time, He was speaking to a man named Nathanael, who had just recognized Him as the Son of God and the King of Israel. Jesus said to Nathanael, "Truly I tell you, you will see heaven opened and the angels of God ascending and descending on the Son of Man" (John 1:51). So, even from the immediate context in John, the title is associated with heavenly things. In the Old Testament, "son of man" can just mean human (see Ps. 8:4: "What is a human being that you remember him, a son of man that you look after him?"). But it's also the way God consistently addressed the prophet, Ezekiel. And, most strikingly, the prophet Daniel saw a vision of "one like a son of man" approaching God Himself and being given an everlasting, universal kingdom (Dan. 7:13–14).

READ DANIEL 7:13-14.

This is most likely the Old Testament context that would have sprung to Nicodemus's mind when Jesus said, "No one has ascended into heaven except the one who descended from heaven—the Son of Man" (John 3:13). Jesus wasn't just a teacher sent by God. He's God's long-promised Messiah: the anointed King whom God's people had been waiting for! He emphasized that truth by drawing on a strange analogy.

What claim did Jesus make in verses 14-15?

READ NUMBERS 21:4-9. Summarize the story and explain why Jesus would have pointed to it in His dialogue with Nicodemus.

This story gives us a clear picture of the ultimate means of escape from God's judgment: Jesus's death on the cross in our place.

This comparison set up the most famous verse in the Bible: "For God loved the world in this way: He gave his one and only Son, so that everyone who believes in him will not perish but have eternal life" (John 3:16). In John's Gospel, we find that having "eternal life" is John's equivalent for seeing or entering "the kingdom of God/heaven" in Matthew, Mark, and Luke. Jesus's first response to Nicodemus: "Truly I tell you, unless someone is born again, he cannot see the kingdom of God" (v. 3) is further explained by John 3:15-16. Jesus's death on the cross is the means by which we can be born again and see His kingdom. Seeing is believing.

How did Nicodemus respond? We are not told in the moment. Instead, John leaves us with a cliff-hanger. But not forever. In John 7, the Pharisees sent officers to arrest Jesus in the temple. But when the officers returned without Jesus and the Pharisees asked them, "Why didn't you bring him?" they replied, "No man ever spoke like this!" (John 7:45-46). The Pharisees responded, "Are you fooled too? Have any of the rulers or Pharisees believed in him? But this crowd, which doesn't know the law, is accursed" (vv. 47-49). But then, Nicodemus spoke up in verses 50-52:

> Nicodemus—the one who came to him previously and who was one of them—said to them, "Our law doesn't judge a man before it hears from him and knows what he's doing, does it?" "You aren't from Galilee too, are you?" they replied. "Investigate and you will see that no prophet arises from Galilee."

Clearly, Nicodemus was wanting to stick up for Jesus. But we still don't know from this passage if he truly believed. However, John gave us one last clue:

READ JOHN 19:38-42.

It seems that Nicodemus may have been like Joseph of Arimathea: a secret disciple. He and Joseph gave Jesus's body a rough-and-ready burial—the best they could do in the short time allowed before the Passover, when all work had to stop. No doubt Nicodemus ultimately heard that Jesus had been raised from the dead, and we have reason to hope that this Pharisee was ultimately "born again."

DAY 2

THE SAMARITAN WOMAN

As we saw yesterday, Jesus's first extended dialogue in John was with a ruler of the Jews—a man of impeccable religious credentials, and one of the seventy men who sat on the Jewish ruling council. His second extended dialogue in John was with someone whose resume could not have been more different. Nicodemus came to Jesus by night, perhaps partly because his reputation could have been damaged if he'd met Jesus in the day. But when Jesus talked with a Samaritan woman at a well, it was in broad daylight. Nicodemus initiated his dialogue with Jesus. But Jesus started the conversation with the Samaritan woman. There are some striking parallels between the two dialogues and some evident contrasts. But where John leaves us in suspense regarding Nicodemus's response, that's not the case with the Samaritan woman at a well. We get to see her eager faith.

Judea (where Jerusalem was located) was in the south, and Galilee (where Jesus was raised and where He began His ministry) was in the north. Samaria lay in-between. Jews often avoided going through this region because of a generations-old hostility between the Jews and the Samaritans. When the original Northern Kingdom of Israel had been conquered by the Assyrians in 722 BC, the Assyrians had deported many of Israel's Jewish inhabitants and resettled people from five other nations in their territory. These immigrants had intermarried with the Jews who'd been allowed to remain in Israel, so the Samaritans were racially mixed and religiously compromised. While they accepted the first five books of the Hebrew Bible, they'd developed their own religious practices, including setting up a temple on Mount Gerizim. In 128 BC, the Jews had destroyed this Samaritan temple, cementing the hostility between the two people groups.

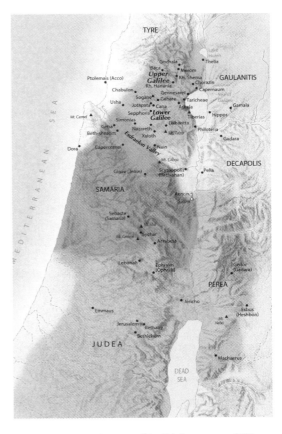

Despite this animosity, Jesus led His disciples right into Samaria on His way back to Galilee. At midday, He sat down at Jacob's well—within sight of Mount Gerizim.

That's when a Samaritan woman came to draw water.

> **READ JOHN 4:1-26.** How did the conversation begin, and what was the Samaritan woman's response (vv. 6-9)?

The issue wasn't just that Jesus was talking with this woman. He was proposing they share a drinking vessel, which most Jewish rabbis would not have dreamed of doing with a Samaritan. The concern wasn't hygiene. It was religious purity. So, Jesus's request was quite shocking.

> In verse 10, how did Jesus respond to the woman's question?

Jesus first said, "Give me a drink." Then, He pointed out that He is the One who is truly in a position to give. The phrase "living water" could mean "fresh water" or "spring water," so the woman quite naturally took Him literally.

> How did the woman respond to Jesus's statement? What were her objections and questions (vv. 11-12)?

Jacob was Abraham's grandson and the father of the twelve sons who went on to be the heads of the twelve tribes of Israel. Both the Jews and the Samaritans saw themselves as the true heirs of Abraham, Isaac, and Jacob. To claim to be greater than Jacob would be a wild assertion.

> What contrast did Jesus draw between the water from Jacob's well and the water He will give (vv. 13-14)?

READ JEREMIAH 2:13; 17:13. How do these verses help us understand what Jesus meant in John 4:14?

This is the fourth time Jesus referenced "eternal life" in John. The first was in His dialogue with Nicodemus. But even with His explanation, the woman's response in verse 15 indicated she was still not tracking with Jesus.

Why do you think she was still struggling to understand?

In verse 16, Jesus said something that probably strikes us as rude—as if He didn't want to talk with this woman in her own right, apart from her husband. But first-century readers might have thought it was about time Jesus did this. It was super inappropriate for Him to be having an extended, private conversation with a woman, let alone a Samaritan woman! But as their conversation progressed, we find that both first-century readers and modern readers misunderstand Jesus's intention when He told her to call her husband.

What does the dialogue in verses 16-18 reveal about her and about Him?

We don't know whether this woman had been divorced by multiple men or whether she'd been serially widowed and was now in a de facto marriage. But in any case, her sexual history is suspicious, adding an extra layer to the inappropriateness of a respectable Jewish rabbi spending time with her. But far from being taken aback by her history or current situation, Jesus knew it from the first, before He even asked her for a drink.

After Jesus shared His knowledge about her situation, she proclaimed Him to be a prophet and shifted the conversation to religious matters.

What theological difference between Jews and Samaritans did she raise for Him to comment on?

How did Jesus show her that this theological difference was soon to be irrelevant (vv. 21-24)?

What happens in the dialogue in verses 25-26 that is both significant and stunning?

This is the first time in John's Gospel that Jesus explicitly confirmed He is the Messiah. It's also the first of his "I am" statements, though this is hard to see in English. His response in the Greek is more literally, "I am, the one speaking to you."[7]

At this mic drop moment, the disciples returned. They were evidently also shocked that Jesus was talking with this woman, but they didn't want to say anything.

What things took place in verses 28-29 that show us something significant has happened in the women's life?

John gave us this evocative detail: the woman left her water jar. She grasped that Jesus was offering her a kind of water better than the life-giving liquid she was used to getting from the well. Then she ran into town to proclaim the news.

What message did the woman have for the people of her town, and how did they respond (vv. 29-30)?

After this extraordinary dialogue with this Samaritan woman, Jesus had a briefer dialogue with His disciples.

READ JOHN 4:31-42.

The Samaritan woman thought Jesus was talking about literal water when He mentioned living water.

What parallel mistake did Jesus's disciples make in verses 31-34?

In verses 35-38, Jesus used another metaphor, comparing a spiritual harvest to a physical one, and told His disciples it was harvest time.

How does this metaphor help us to understand what happened in verses 39-42?

Nicodemus came as a representative of the Pharisees—one of the most religious groups of Jews—and he was one of only a few who were saved from that group. This sexually compromised and socially marginalized Samaritan woman became an unintentional representative of her whole Samaritan town, and many from her town believed in Jesus as Savior of the world. Jesus engaged in a push and pull conversation with both this woman and Nicodemus. Both were humbled: Nicodemus by having his ability to be a teacher of Israel called into question and the Samaritan woman by having her marital history revealed. Both were confronted with a metaphor, which they at first didn't understand. Both ultimately came to follow Jesus. But amazingly, Jesus had His longest, private, recorded conversation in the Gospels with the Samaritan woman, not with the ruler of the Jews.

Use the following questions to spend some time reflecting on Jesus's conversation with this most unlikely dialogue partner:

What does it say about Jesus that He knew all of her history and still wanted to talk with her?

What does it say about Jesus that He knows your history and mine and still longs to give us everlasting life with Him?

DAY 3

THE CANAANITE WOMAN

John's Gospel is known for capturing some of Jesus's extended dialogues with individuals. But we see individual dialogues in the other Gospels too. A remarkable example that's recorded in both Matthew and Mark is another interaction Jesus had with a non-Jewish woman. Like in His conversations with Nicodemus and with the Samaritan woman, Jesus introduced a metaphor. But unlike Nicodemus and the Samaritan woman, this Gentile woman picked up on it at once and ran with it—despite the fact that it required her to humble herself.

In both Matthew and Mark, this dialogue followed a confrontation Jesus had with the Pharisees and scribes who had come to Jesus from Jerusalem (see Matt. 15:1; Mark 7:1). These hyper-religious Jews were criticizing Jesus because His disciples were not following the rules of ceremonial washing prescribed by their tradition. But Jesus pushed back. He called them hypocrites, quoted the prophet Isaiah against them, and accused them of encouraging people to break the fifth of the Ten Commandments: "Honor your father and your mother" (Matt. 15:4). Jesus then explained to His disciples that it's what comes out of your heart that makes you unclean, not the food you put into your mouth. Mark commented that by saying this, Jesus declared all foods to be clean (Mark 7:19). This tore down one of the dividing lines between Jews and Gentiles. It's vital we have this context in our minds as we come to Jesus's dialogue with a Gentile woman.

READ MATTHEW 15:21-28. Where did Jesus go to in verse 21?

Tyre was a city about thirty-five miles northwest of Galilee, on the Mediterranean coast.[8] In the Hebrew scriptures, Tyre was associated with paganism and idolatry. Multiple Old Testament prophets prophesied against Tyre (Isa. 23; Ezek. 26–28; Amos 1:9-10; Zech. 9:2-3). Sidon was twenty-two miles north of Tyre, had a similar reputation, and was also preached against by the prophets.[9] What's more, the most notorious queen in Israel's history, Queen Jezebel, had come from Sidon and promoted Baal worship. Suffice it to say, Tyre and Sidon weren't just Gentile cities. They were Gentile cities especially known for their sinfulness. But this is the region to which Jesus headed, after His confrontation with the Jerusalem-based Pharisees and scribes.

How did Matthew describe the woman who came to Jesus (15:22)?

The Canaanites were the pagan people originally inhabiting the promised land. They had been progressively conquered by God's people after the Israelites' escape from Egypt and their forty-years of wandering in the wilderness. By Jesus's day, the Canaanites were no longer a distinct people group. In fact, Mark's Gospel calls this woman "Syrophonecian." But Matthew's use of "Canaanite" emphasized that this woman was an ethnic and religious outsider to Israel.

How did this woman address Jesus?

"Son of David" was a title with messianic overtones. Matthew's Gospel begins: "An account of the genealogy of Jesus Christ, the Son of David, the Son of Abraham" (1:1). It did not only mean the Messiah. Jesus's adoptive father, Joseph, was addressed as "son of David" by the angel who told him to go ahead and marry Mary, despite her unexpected pregnancy (v. 20). But when Jesus healed a demon-possessed man in Matthew 12 and the astonished crowds asked, "Could this be the Son of David?" they were definitely wondering if they'd just seen God's promised King in action (v. 23). So, when this Canaanite woman called Jesus "Son of David," it suggests she had some sense of who He is.

Why did this woman need Jesus's help, and how did He initially respond?

Jesus's non-responsiveness was emphasized in the passage. He didn't answer her with a single word. Crickets. The way the disciples described this woman suggests she was being very persistent—pleading and pleading and not giving up.

How did Jesus answer in Matthew 15:24?

Rather than responding to the disciple's request, it seems Jesus responded to the woman. In Matthew 10, Jesus had summoned His twelve apostles, given them authority over unclean spirits and sicknesses, and issued these instructions:

Don't take the road that leads to the Gentiles, and don't enter any
Samaritan town. Instead, go to the lost sheep of the house of Israel.
As you go, proclaim, "The kingdom of heaven has come near." Heal
the sick, raise the dead, cleanse those with leprosy, drive out demons.

MATTHEW 10:5b-8a

Here, in conversation with this non-Jewish woman, Jesus asserted the priority of
His mission to the Jews. But we know from earlier in Matthew that Jesus did not
turn away from Gentiles who approached Him. In Matthew 8, a Roman centurion
had asked Jesus to come and heal his sick servant. But when Jesus offered to go
with him, the centurion had declared himself unworthy to have Jesus come under
his roof. He asked Jesus just to say the word, believing his servant would be
healed based on Jesus's authority. Jesus was so impressed with this man's faith
that He told His followers,

Truly I tell you, I have not found anyone in Israel with so great a faith.
I tell you that many will come from east and west to share the banquet
with Abraham, Isaac, and Jacob in the kingdom of heaven. But the sons
of the kingdom will be thrown into the outer darkness where there will
be weeping and gnashing of teeth.

MATTHEW 8:10b-12

With this background in mind, Jesus's claim that He was sent only to the lost
sheep of the house of Israel sounds more like a challenge to the woman—akin to
His claim to Nicodemus that if Nicodemus wanted to see the kingdom of God he
must be born again.

How did the woman respond (Matt. 15:25)?

This simple prayer has become a go-to for me. I love how this woman got right
in front of Jesus, knelt down and begged. Often, when I'm under stress, I'll take
a leaf out of her book and just pray three words: "Lord, help me!" She'd just
heard Jesus saying He was only there for Jews. But she was determined that He
was going to make an exception. Jesus's reaction pressed her still further.

What did Jesus say in verse 26, and what is your initial reaction to His words?

In the Old Testament, the Israelites were often referred to as God's children. *Dogs* was a pejorative term that Jews sometimes used to refer to Gentiles. The word Jesus used was associated with dogs kept as family pets rather than scavenging dogs, but it's still not a compliment.[10]

Let's pause here for a moment. Jesus's response feels super jarring, and it's meant to. But we know from His encounter with the Roman centurion that Jesus isn't anti-Gentile. He was pushing her to make a point.

We might expect this Gentile woman to be offended by Jesus's metaphor. But instead, she picked it up and ran with it.

What argument did the woman make in verse 27, and how did it reveal her great humility?

How did Jesus respond to her (v. 28)?

As with Nicodemus and the Samaritan woman, we see Jesus engaging in push and pull in this dialogue with the Canaanite woman. But unlike them, she grasped Jesus's metaphor from the first, just as she came to Him humbly from the first.

Take a moment to ponder her example. How can you apply this to your own relationship with Jesus?

What do we learn about Jesus from this dialogue with the Canaanite woman?

How does Matthew and Mark including the dialogue make this story more impactful than just summarizing it?

DAY 4

SIMON THE PHARISEE

In Nicodemus, we saw a rare example of a Pharisee coming to Jesus with a true desire to learn. In Luke's Gospel, we read about another Pharisee who made an atypical choice. Instead of criticizing Jesus for whom He was eating with, this Pharisee invited Jesus to dinner at his house. But as the dialogue around the table unfolded, we see this man—whose name was Simon—failing to see who Jesus is, while a most unlikely person rises to the role he should have played.

The context of the dialogue in Luke 7 is Jesus reflecting on the ministry of John the Baptist. Luke stated that when all the people and the tax collectors heard what Jesus was saying, "they acknowledged God's way of righteousness, because they had been baptized with John's baptism" (v. 29). By contrast, "since the Pharisees and experts in the law had not been baptized by him, they rejected the plan of God for themselves" (v. 30).

Jesus then reflected on how both He and John the Baptist couldn't win:

> John the Baptist did not come eating bread or drinking wine, and you say, "He has a demon!" The Son of Man has come eating and drinking, and you say, "Look, a glutton and a drunkard, a friend of tax collectors and sinners!"

LUKE 7:33-34

Following that, Luke told the story of a Pharisee who invited Jesus to dinner.

READ LUKE 7:36-50.

Jesus accepted a meal invitation from Simon the Pharisee. The fact that they were reclining at the table indicates this was a special meal, not just an everyday affair. As they were eating, a woman arrived at Simon's house.

How was the woman described, and what actions did she take?

While Luke described her as "a sinner," we don't know exactly what form this woman's sin took. It's possible she was a prostitute or that she was well-known for sinning in some other way. At special meals like the one to which Simon had invited Jesus, it was normal for the doors to be left open, so folks who had not been invited could sit around the walls and listen to the conversation. The appearance of an uninvited guest would not have been surprising. But this woman's identity and her actions were.

> Summarize Simon the Pharisee's response when he saw what this woman was doing (v. 39).

Though the Pharisee talked to himself—under his breath or in his mind—Jesus confronted him with a mini parable about a money lender and two debtors.

> What was the gist of the story, and what was the point in Jesus telling it?

A denarius was a standard daily wage, so a debt of five hundred denarii would have been a massive debt from the point of view of the average Jew of Jesus's day—the kind of debt a person could never hope to pay. Simon correctly understood the meaning of the story but was likely taken aback by Jesus's application of the parable.

> In verse 44, toward whom did Jesus turn, and what did He ask Simon?

The reality is that Simon did see this woman. But he saw her very differently from how Jesus saw her. Jesus went on to make a point-by-point comparison between Simon and the sinful woman.

Fill in this table:

WHAT HAD SIMON FAILED TO DO?	WHAT HAD THE WOMAN DONE?

How did Jesus conclude His conversation with Simon, and how did the conclusion reveal the identities of the two debtors in His parable?

How did Jesus's response to the woman reveal the identity of the moneylender in the parable?

How did the other dinner guests respond to Jesus's declaration (v. 49)?

In Luke 5, Jesus was confronted with a paralyzed man, who had been lowered down to Him by his friends through a hole in the roof of the house where Jesus was teaching. Jesus had said to him, "your sins are forgiven," and the scribes and Pharisees had thought to themselves, "Who is this man who speaks blasphemies? Who can forgive sins but God alone?" (vv. 20-21). Jesus went on to prove His authority to forgive sins by healing the paralyzed man. But the woman in Luke 7 did not come to Him for healing but forgiveness.

How does Jesus finally respond to the woman in Luke 7:50?

Simon the Pharisee thought he held the moral high ground over this notoriously sinful woman. But Jesus showed him he did not. She'd been completely forgiven for her sin. But Simon's failure to recognize his need for Jesus and his resultant failure to welcome Jesus properly into his home revealed he may not have been forgiven at all. He thought he had less sin to be forgiven than the woman did. What's interesting is that Jesus didn't argue that point. Instead, He lifted this woman up as an example of love.

This dialogue began with Jesus and Simon the Pharisee. But Jesus's last words are spoken to the woman, whom Simon deemed to be beneath his contempt. She came to Jesus humbly, willing to endure humiliation to show her heartfelt gratitude. Ultimately, that's the only way we can come to Jesus and be received by Him. But if we do—like her He'll lift us up.

DAY 5

SIMON PETER

My guess is you know what it feels like to be let down by a friend. Maybe it was in middle school when someone you thought was one of your besties suddenly decided to switch groups and cut you out. Perhaps it was much more recently. Maybe a close friend made in adulthood, someone you deeply trusted and thought was on your side mysteriously ghosted you or did something that really hurt you and betrayed your trust.

The four dialogues we've looked at so far this week are with people who were not among Jesus's itinerant disciples. Today, we'll explore a conversation Jesus had with one of His closest friends: Simon Peter. It's the last dialogue recorded in John's Gospel, and it's deeply moving. In this conversation, we see Jesus reconnecting with a friend who had denied knowing Him three times.

Before Jesus's arrest, Peter had promised Jesus that he would lay down his life for Him if that was what it took to follow Him. Jesus had replied, "Will you lay down your life for me? Truly I tell you, a rooster will not crow until you have denied me three times" (John 13:38). In Matthew's account, we hear that Peter made an even bolder statement, claiming that even if all the other disciples fell away, he never would (Matt. 26:33). All four Gospels record Peter's catastrophic failure to follow through on what he'd promised. But only John recorded the conversation in which Jesus restored Peter as a leader in the church.

The dialogue we'll look at today took place after Jesus had been raised. Simon Peter decided to go fishing, and some of the other disciples joined him. They fished all night but caught nothing. Then, at daybreak, Jesus called to them and told them to cast their nets on the other side of the boat, and they caught so many fish they weren't able to haul their nets in. Once Peter realized the one calling to them from shore was Jesus, he jumped into the sea—presumably to swim to shore and get to Jesus as quickly as he could. Jesus already had breakfast cooked for them. When they'd finished breakfast, Jesus asked Peter a question.

READ JOHN 21:15-19. What question did Jesus ask Peter in verse 15?

How did Peter respond?

What did Jesus commission Peter to do (v. 15)?

We might have thought that Peter's epic failure to follow through on his promise of dying with Jesus and not even acknowledge he knew Jesus at all would disqualify him from any kind of leadership in Jesus's kingdom. But this command to feed Jesus's lambs suggests Peter was, in fact, being entrusted with a pastoral role.

Fill in the chart showing the dialogue between Jesus and Peter in verses 15-17.

VERSE	JESUS'S QUESTION	PETER'S RESPONSE	JESUS'S COMMAND
Verse 15			
Verse 16			

(continued on the next page)

VERSE	JESUS'S QUESTION	PETER'S RESPONSE	JESUS'S COMMAND
Verse 17			

In view of their history, why do you think Jesus asked Peter the same question three times?

In this conversation, Jesus gave Peter the chance to retrace his steps on the fateful night when he denied even knowing Jesus three times. Now Peter had the opportunity to affirm his love for Jesus three times instead. Jesus had predicted Peter would deny him, but Peter hadn't believed Jesus. Now, he affirmed that Jesus knows all things—not just in general, but in particular the things of Peter's heart. It's evidently a painful conversation for Peter. But it's also one in which Jesus affirmed that He was still planning to use Peter in powerful ways, despite Peter's dramatic failure.

How does this conversation reassure you when you think of the times you've most dramatically let Jesus down?

What was the meaning of the prophecy Jesus spoke over Peter (vv. 18-19)?

How did this give Peter a second chance to follow through on his original promise?

Right before Peter's original claim to follow Jesus to the death and Jesus's original prediction that Peter wouldn't follow through, they had this exchange: "'Lord,' Simon Peter said to him, 'where are you going?' Jesus answered, 'Where I am going you cannot follow me now, but you will follow later'" (John 13:36).

How does this help us understand Jesus's command to Peter, "Follow me" (John 21:19)?

Peter was one of Jesus's closest disciples. He thought he had the courage it would take to follow Jesus even to the death. But he found out he didn't. So, when the resurrected Jesus met Peter for this poignant dialogue, Peter was freshly humbled. He wasn't the man he thought he was. He'd denied he knew Jesus three times. But in this exchange, Jesus lovingly reinstated him, commissioned him to lead, and revealed that in the future, Peter would have the opportunity to follow Jesus even unto death as Peter had first promised.

Which dialogue we looked at this week struck you the most? Why?

How do the dialogues we've looked at this week help you see that we can only come to Jesus humbly?

How does the push and pull we see in many of Jesus's dialogues help us to understand the times when Jesus challenges us?

How do these one-on-one conversations we've seen Jesus have help us see He is interested in a one-on-one relationship with each of us?

UNDERSTANDING DIALOGUE

IN THE GOSPELS >

Tips

> Jesus often taught through specific conversations either with His disciples or with strangers or opponents.

> Some dialogues in the Gospels are between Jesus and one other individual while others are between Jesus and a group. Sometimes, one Gospel author will record a dialogue with a group (for example, the disciples or the Pharisees) while another will tell the same story and name the individual who was speaking on behalf of the group.

> Jesus's dialogues forge connection between Himself and the person to whom He was talking.

> Jesus's dialogues frame action and help the onlookers understand what He was doing.

> Jesus's dialogues typically feature some kind of tension, as He engaged in a push and pull with His interlocutor.

> Jesus's dialogues tend to force a reaction, either positive or negative.

> As we read Jesus's dialogues, we should put ourselves in the shoes of different people in the story to see what we can learn from listening in.

Exercise

Below is a passage that features a dialogue Jesus had with Pontius Pilate. Read through the conversation and then, using what you've learned about dialogue, answer the questions that follow.

READ JOHN 18:33-40. Here we see Jesus in dialogue with the Roman governor Pilate, who had the authority to have Jesus crucified.

How does Jesus's response to Pilate's first question raise tension?

What action (if any) does Jesus take in this dialogue?

How do Jesus's words explain His inaction?

What is Pilate's reaction to Jesus, and what does it show about him?

Prophecy

As I was starting work yesterday morning, my eleven-year-old daughter Miranda was unloading the dishwasher and blaring out the song, "We Don't Talk About Bruno." If you're one of the few humans alive today who hasn't heard this song, consider yourself lucky! It's about a character in the Disney film *Encanto* who has the gift (or curse) of being able to see into the future. Various other characters in the film blame Bruno for the mishaps in their lives because he told them what was going to happen.

I think if you grabbed a person off the street and asked him to tell you what prophecy means, he'd probably describe someone like Bruno—a person who can make an accurate prediction about some future event. There's certainly an element of this in biblical prophecy. But often, it's not that straightforward. Biblical prophets spoke on behalf of God. As well as predicting the future, they interpreted the past and described the present, with their future predictions often dependent on how their hearers reacted to the message. For instance, the prophet Jonah was actively upset when the people of Nineveh repented and God did not follow through on the judgment Jonah had been sent to prophesy about. What's more, God often spoke to and through prophets in poetry, so their message was not as straightforward as the message God gave to Jonah: "In forty days Nineveh will be demolished!" (Jonah 3:4).

When it comes to the Gospels, we see the full range of prophetic possibilities at play. We see direct predictions both made and fulfilled. We see prophetic poetry spoken and realized. We see Old Testament passages that do not look like forward-looking prophecies being applied by Gospel authors to the events they're narrating. We see apocalyptic pronouncements being made and apocalyptic visions starting to be fulfilled. Each day this week, we'll explore one strand of this complex tapestry. But we'll also recognize that the various strands are often woven together, so we shouldn't get fixated on neat categories. Instead, we must follow the Gospel authors as they lead us and be open at times to sitting in the tension of uncertainty.

SESSION *Seven*

To access the video teaching sessions, use the instructions in the back of your Bible study book.

NOTES

Watch Rebecca's Session Seven video.

Download the *Navigating Gospel Truth* leader guide at **lifeway.com/gospeltruth**

GROUP DISCUSSION GUIDE

When you hear the word *prophecy*, what do you think? Why do you have that reaction?

What is one prophecy in the Gospels that is confusing or difficult for you to understand? Why?

Which type of prophecy—prediction, poetry, personification, and apocalyptic—is easiest for you to recognize and understand? Why?

Why is it important to recognize and understand how prophecy is used in the Gospels?

What part of the video teaching was most important for you?

DAY 1

PREDICTION

As we saw in our first week of study, after Jesus rose from the dead, He appeared first to some of the women among His disciples—most famously, Mary Magdalene. But later that same day, He appeared to two of His disciples as they walked on the road to a village named Emmaus. He joined their conversation as they processed the crucifixion and the women's testimony of seeing a vision of angels who proclaimed Jesus was alive again. The traveling pair seemed not to have known what to think about the women's story because some of the male disciples had been to the tomb and found it empty but hadn't seen Jesus. We don't know Jesus's tone of voice when He responded. Maybe He was exasperated. Maybe He was shaking His head and sighing. But He said to them,

> "How foolish you are, and how slow to believe all that the prophets have spoken! Wasn't it necessary for the Messiah to suffer these things and enter into his glory?" Then beginning with Moses and all the Prophets, he interpreted for them the things concerning himself in all the Scriptures.

LUKE 24:25-27

Even after saying this, it was not until Jesus sat down for a meal with them and broke the bread that they recognized Him—at which point He disappeared (v. 31)!

Evidently, Jesus pointed them to prophecy about His life, death, and resurrection all over the Old Testament. But even without this Scriptural arsenal, Jesus's disciples should have known He would die and rise again because He had specifically predicted it.

READ LUKE 9:18-24. What happened immediately before Jesus predicted His death in this passage?

What specific things did Jesus predict in verse 22?

How do verses 23-24 build on Jesus's direct prediction of His death and resurrection?

Jesus did not specify in His original prediction He would die on a cross, but He implied that means of death in verse 23. Jesus's second prediction of His death in Luke 9 is more enigmatic. Jesus had performed a miracle, and the people were amazed. But while everyone was marveling at Jesus's power, He jolted His disciples with an unwelcome prediction.

READ LUKE 9:44-45. How did Jesus emphasize the importance of His disciples taking in what He was saying?

How did Luke emphasize the disciples' failure to grasp His meaning?

Jesus's third prediction of His death in Luke was specific and direct. But His disciples still didn't get it.

READ LUKE 18:31-33. How is this prediction different than the first two?

How is it similar?

Jesus predicted His death three times in Matthew and Mark as well (see Matt. 16:21-23; 17:22-23; 20:17-19 and Mark 8:31-33; 9:30-31; 10:32-34). Matthew's account of Jesus's third prediction is the most specific:

> While going up to Jerusalem, Jesus took the twelve disciples aside privately and said to them on the way, "See, we are going up to Jerusalem. The Son of Man will be handed over to the chief priests and scribes, and they will condemn him to death. They will hand him over to the Gentiles to be mocked, flogged, and crucified, and on the third day he will be raised."

MATTHEW 20:17-19

Matthew didn't tell us how the disciples reacted to this detailed prophecy. But immediately after this prediction, Matthew told how the mother of the sons of Zebedee (the apostles James and John) came to Jesus and asked Him for top spots in His kingdom for her sons. When the other ten apostles heard about this, they were angry. But Jesus explained that leadership in His kingdom isn't about lording it over others but about serving them. He concluded with another prediction of His death.

READ MATTHEW 20:25-28. How did Jesus predict His death again in these verses?

How did Jesus interpret His death in verse 28?

In the previous instances, Jesus made specific and straightforward predictions about Himself. So, when we look back at Old Testament prophecy about Him, we tend to expect the same approach, and sometimes, that's how it works. For example, in Matthew 2, wise men come to Jerusalem from the east, saying, "Where is he who has been born king of the Jews? For we saw his star at its rising and have come to worship him" (v. 2). Herod, the puppet king the Romans had set up over the Jews, was disturbed when he heard about this. He wasn't keen on the idea of another "king of the Jews." So, he asked the chief priests and the scribes where the Messiah was supposed to be born. They replied by quoting from the prophet Micah:

> "In Bethlehem of Judea," they told him, "because this is what was written by the prophet: And you, Bethlehem, in the land of Judah, are by no means least among the rulers of Judah: Because out of you will come a ruler who will shepherd my people Israel."

MATTHEW 2:5-6

This quotation from Micah had an original context: the Assyrian invasion of 701 BC. But it also pointed forward to the ultimate Messiah, who would save His people not from the Assyrians, or even from the Romans, but from their sins (Matt. 1:21).

This is the second time Matthew explicitly quoted an Old Testament prophecy being fulfilled by Jesus. It was specific and straightforward. But the first time Matthew did this, it's not quite as clear, and we may find ourselves more confused.

READ MATTHEW 1:18-25. What name did the angel of the Lord tell Joseph he should give to Mary's Spirit-conceived son?

What name does the prophecy from Isaiah, which Matthew claimed was being fulfilled here, specify?

You might be thinking, "Wait a minute, Jesus wasn't named Immanuel! So how can His birth be a fulfillment of that prophecy?" Understand that in this poetic space, names aren't just literal names; they're also titles. Matthew was deliberately making the point that Jesus—who was given that name meaning "God saves" because He will save His people from their sins (Matt. 1:21)—is also the One who is Immanuel: "God with us." This first quotation in Matthew points us to the fact that when Old Testament Scriptures are fulfilled in the New Testament, it typically isn't a straightforward, specific prediction coming true. Like the sacrificial lambs in the Old Testament foreshadowing Jesus's true sacrifice, we'll often need New Testament interpretation—like John the Baptist pointing to Jesus and saying, "Look, the Lamb of God, who takes away the sin of the world!" (John 1:29)—to understand how Jesus is fulfilling Old Testament Scripture.

DAY 2

POETRY

Had I the heavens' embroidered cloths,
Enwrought with golden and silver light,
The blue and the dim and the dark cloths
Of night and light and the half light,
I would spread the cloths under your feet:
But I, being poor, have only my dreams;
I have spread my dreams under your feet;
Tread softly because you tread on my dreams.[1]

This is one of my favorite poems. It's by the Irish poet W. B. Yeats, and I find it very beautiful. Poetry can woo our hearts in ways most other forms of speech cannot, and the Bible is chock full of it.

You may be wondering why we're spending a day of study on prophecy in the Gospels thinking about poetry. After all, large swaths of the poetry in the Bible are not prophecy, and not all prophecy is delivered in poetic form. But since there is a lot of overlap between prophecy and poetry in the Scriptures, it's worth taking some time getting a handle on what we should expect from poetry. Doing so will help us be ready to tune into prophecy without finding ourselves frustrated—like when you're trying to tune into a radio station from your car stereo and not finding the right frequency.

Even within our own culture, defining what counts as poetry is notoriously hard. Poetry written in English can take specific forms. For example, sonnets are poems composed of fourteen lines with a specific structure both for their rhythm and their rhyme scheme. All sonnets are poems. But not all poems are sonnets! Some poems in English don't follow any particular structure and are only recognizable as poetry, as opposed to prose, because of how they're written on the page. However, most poems in English do follow some sort of structure when it comes to rhythm and rhyme, and they often major on metaphor and other forms of non-literal communication. But asking, "What is a poem?" is like asking, "What is art?"

When it comes to biblical poetry, there also aren't hard-and-fast rules, but there are common features we can look for. Rhyming is far less characteristic of biblical poetry than it is of poetry in English—which is good news for us, as rhyme is almost always lost in translation. Instead, Hebrew poetry trades in parallelism, meaning ideas in one verse or couple of verses are repeated, contrasted, or developed in the next. But one thing poetry in our culture has in common with biblical poetry is the central place of metaphor. When David began Psalm 23 with, "The LORD is my shepherd," we instinctively tune into the fact that he was writing a poem.

We find two prophetic poems in the first chapter of Luke's Gospel—one delivered by Jesus's mother, Mary, and the other by John the Baptist's father, Zechariah.

READ LUKE 1:46-55.

The first two lines of Mary's poem give us an example of parallelism: the second line repeats the ideas of the first line in different words.

> Circle the words or phrases in the second line that correspond to words or phrases in the first line:
>
> My soul magnifies the Lord,
>
> and my spirit rejoices in God my Savior.

This is sometimes called synonymous parallelism because we find synonyms for words in the first line in the second: for example, soul/spirit. But Mary's speech also gives us examples of antithetical parallelism, where the second line contrasts with the first.

READ VERSES 52-53 AGAIN. What examples of antithetical parallelism do you see in these verses?

Mary's poem includes direct prediction. In verse 48 she said, "from now on all generations will call me blessed"—and that prediction has certainly come true.

But much of her speech looks back to what God has done. Something we'll notice as we explore Old Testament passages that are claimed prophetically in the New Testament is that poetic declarations about past events are often applied prophetically to future events. Mary's speech fits this model. From her own experience of God choosing her—a no-name, low-income girl from an insignificant town—she recognized God as the One who works great reversals, past, present, and future.

Zechariah's speech is explicitly tagged as prophecy (Luke 1:67). He made specific future predictions.

READ LUKE 1:67-79. What metaphor did Zechariah introduce in verse 69?

In the Old Testament, the horn was a symbol of strength and salvation. For example, in Psalm 18, David declared:

> The LORD is my rock, my fortress, and my deliverer, my God, my rock where I seek refuge, my shield and the horn of my salvation, my stronghold.

PSALM 18:2

What prediction did Zechariah make about his son, who would grow up to be John the Baptist (Luke 1:76-77)?

What metaphors do you see in verses 78-79?

Zechariah envisaged God's salvation as being like the rising of the sun at dawn, scattering the darkness and enabling people who are sitting under death's shadow to stand up and walk on the path of peace. The third poetic declaration in Luke's Gospel was delivered in the temple by a man named Simeon, and it builds on themes also found in Mary and Zechariah's poems.

READ LUKE 2:29-32. What words and ideas from Zechariah's speech do you see echoed in Simeon's?

In Matthew's Gospel, we see similar poetic imagery being applied to Jesus. But rather than it coming in the form of new poems drawing on Old Testament themes, Matthew mines directly from the prophet Isaiah.

READ MATTHEW 4:12-17. What specific event in Jesus's life did Matthew use to tie Him to Isaiah's prophecy?

Where do you see parallelism in this quotation from Isaiah?

What metaphors do you see in this passage that were also present in our passages from Luke?

If you and I went back in time two thousand years and visited the territory of Zebulun and Naphtali before and after Jesus moved to Capernaum, we would not have noticed a change in the climatic conditions. The amount of darkness to light would have remained seasonally the same. But Jesus is the Light of the world, and His presence there would have been like daybreak in spiritual terms.

READ ISAIAH 9:1-7. How does the rest of Isaiah's prophecy, even beyond what Matthew quoted, point to Jesus?

Matthew began his Gospel with the claim that Jesus is God's long-promised King, the son of David (Matt. 1:1). In Matthew 4, he quoted a poetic prophecy about One who would reign on the throne of David and over His kingdom forever. When the Gospel authors cited Old Testament prophecy, they typically expected their readers to bring to mind the passage even beyond what they had directly quoted. Matthew evidently expected us to bring the rest of Isaiah's poetic prophecy in Isaiah 9 to bear on Jesus here.

PERSONIFICATION

Yesterday, we looked at metaphor and parallelism as two characteristics of biblical poetry. Today, we're going to look at another feature of biblical poetry and prophecy called *personification*. Personification is when an author describes a non-human being, thing, or idea as if it was human. One famous example of personification is in the book of Proverbs, where Wisdom is personified as a woman, calling out in the streets (1:20). Here, an abstract idea is personified.

We also see the personification of natural phenomena; for example, Psalm 98 declares, "Let the rivers clap their hands; let the mountains shout together for joy" (v. 8). Rivers don't have hands, and mountains can't shout! But the psalmist was using personification to describe how the natural world should respond to the Lord. In that same psalm, we see God Himself personified:

> Sing a new song to the LORD, for he has performed wonders; his right hand and holy arm have won him victory.

PSALM 98:1

God is spirit. He does not have a literal right hand or an arm. But here God is personified as a mighty warrior.

We've already encountered personification in our study of the Gospels. When we looked at Jesus the bridegroom, we noticed that in the Old Testament, God is frequently pictured as a loving, faithful Husband, and Israel as His often-unfaithful wife. Hosea was one of the prophets especially known for his use of the marriage metaphor. But in Hosea 11, rather than picturing God's people as a wife, we find another personification.

READ HOSEA 11:1-3. How did the Lord personify Israel in these verses?

What event in Israel's history did God point to in verse 1?

According to verse 2, how did Israel react to being called by God?

In verse 3, God referred to Ephraim, one of Joseph's sons. He became the head of the northern tribes, and his name is sometimes used as a synonym for the Northern Kingdom of Israel.

How did God flesh out the personification of Israel (aka Ephraim) as His young child (v. 3)?

What do we learn about God's relationship with Israel from this personification?

In Matthew 2, we read about wise men from the east going to Jerusalem in search of the King of the Jews and being sent to Bethlehem to find Him. After they found the infant Jesus, God warned them in a dream not to go back to Jerusalem and report to King Herod what they'd found. Then, God sent an angel in a dream to Joseph with a warning and instruction.

READ MATTHEW 2:13-15. What were God's instructions to Joseph?

How did Matthew connect this event in Jesus's early life to Hosea 11?

King Herod died not long after ordering the slaughter of the baby and toddler boys in Jerusalem, so Jesus was likely still a young child when His parents left Egypt. How does this resonate with the personification of Israel in Hosea 11?

Was Hosea's original prophecy predicting the future or interpreting the past?

When Matthew connected Jesus's time in Egypt as a young child to Hosea's prophecy, he wasn't pointing to a prediction that had come true. He was pointing to Jesus as the true Israel.

If we read through the Gospels with an eye on Old Testament connections, one of the things we'll notice is the ways in which Jesus's life mirrored the history of God's people. God's people were called out of Egypt and so was Jesus. God parted the waters of the Red Sea so His people could pass through, and Jesus passed through the waters at His baptism (Matt. 3:13-17). After passing through the Red Sea, God's people spent forty years in the wilderness. After His baptism, Jesus spent forty days and forty nights in the wilderness, being tempted by Satan (Matt. 4:1-11). Israel was pictured as God's son. But Jesus is God's true Son, embodying God's true people. Personification is a poetic device. But Jesus, in a real sense, personifies God's people. We see this flowing out into New Testament theology, as the church is pictured as Jesus's body here on earth.

Let's look at one more example of personification from Matthew 2.

READ MATTHEW 2:16-18. What do you think is the example of personification in this passage?

When King Herod learned that the wise men who came to Jerusalem looking for an alternative King of the Jews had not come back and informed him about the location of this new King, he was furious. So, knowing that the magi had been pointed to Bethlehem, he had all the male children two years and under in Bethlehem killed.

That prompted Matthew to record these words:

> Then what was spoken through Jeremiah the prophet was fulfilled: A voice was heard in Ramah, weeping, and great mourning, Rachel weeping for her children; and she refused to be consoled, because they are no more.

MATTHEW 2:17-18

Ramah was about five miles north of Jerusalem. Bethlehem was about five miles to the south. Rachel was the second wife of Jacob and the mother of his last two sons: Joseph and Benjamin. She died hundreds of years before Jeremiah's prophecy and well over a thousand years before King Herod had the baby boys of Bethlehem slaughtered. So, how was this horrific event fulfilling Jeremiah's words about Rachel? As one of the matriarchs of God's people, Rachel stood in as a personification of Jewish mothers lamenting their dead sons—both in Jeremiah's time and in Jesus's.

In Matthew 21, we see another example of Old Testament personification being fulfilled.

READ MATTHEW 21:1-9. Matthew quoted from the prophet Zechariah, who declared:

Rejoice greatly, Daughter Zion! Shout in triumph, Daughter Jerusalem!
Look, your King is coming to you; he is righteous and victorious, humble and riding on a donkey, on a colt, the foal of a donkey.

ZECHARIAH 9:9

Where do you see synonymous parallelism in this verse?

Where do you see personification?

In Zechariah's prophecy, the "Daughter of Zion/Jerusalem" was a personification of Jerusalem as a whole. In what ways do we see Zechariah's prophecy fulfilled as Jesus went into Jerusalem?

People sometimes say that Christians have made God in their own image. But the Bible tells us the opposite: God has made us in His image and His likeness.

How has this study of personification helped you understand more about Jesus, who is the true flesh-and-blood image of the invisible God (Col. 1:15)?

DAY 4

APOCALYPTIC

The 2022 film *Moonfall* is one of many films that could be categorized as "apocalyptic." It's a sci-fi disaster film, which imagines a world in which the moon has been knocked out of its orbit and is now on a collision course with earth. The film was one of the most expensive independent films ever made, and it totally bombed. I like to think that when the filmmakers realized how much money it had lost, they looked at one another and said, "Well, it's not the end of the world!"

We tend to use that expression to put bad things in perspective. Not really tragic things, but things that didn't pan out as we'd hoped. Like, "I'm sad our vacation got canceled, but it's not the end of the world." In popular culture, the end of the world is definitely seen as a bad thing. But in the Bible, we see the end of the world as we know it—or judgment day—as an event that is both good and bad. For God's people, it's very good. For those who have rejected God, it's the worst day imaginable.

In our study today, we're going to look at passages in the Gospels that can be called apocalyptic. The word *apocalypse* comes from the Greek word *apokalyptein*, which means "to uncover."[2] The last book in the Bible is generally known as the book of Revelation. But sometimes, it's called the Apocalypse of John. So, what is revealed in the book of Revelation and other apocalyptic passages of Scripture? God's endgame.

Like other forms of prophecy, the biblical genre known as apocalyptic is highly poetic. It's filled with imagery and personifications. We've seen glimpses of apocalyptic writing in our studies already. When we talked about Jesus the bridegroom, we dipped into the book of Revelation and heard what sounded like the voice of a vast multitude shouting out,

> Hallelujah, because our Lord God, the Almighty, reigns! Let us be glad, rejoice, and give him glory, because the marriage of the Lamb has come, and his bride has prepared herself.

REVELATION 19:6b-7

We also saw the apocalyptic genre in action when we read from the prophet Daniel's vision of one "like a son of man." Let's go back to that passage for a moment so that it's fresh in our minds as we look at Jesus's words about Himself in Matthew 26.

READ DANIEL 7:13-14. In Daniel's vision, how did the one like a son of man appear before the Ancient of Days?

READ MATTHEW 24:1-28. What prediction did Jesus make in verse 2?

This prediction was fulfilled in AD 70 when the Romans attacked Jerusalem and destroyed the temple. This was an absolutely catastrophic event in Jewish history. During the Romans' siege on Jerusalem, thousands of Jews were crucified outside the city walls in an attempt to pressure those inside to surrender. The Jewish-Roman historian Josephus claimed that over a million died in the conquest.[3] While historians have since shown that this must be an exaggerated number, it speaks to the utter devastation the Jewish people in Jerusalem and Judea experienced. The truly horrific nature of this event means that it is sometimes hard to distinguish between Jesus's predictions about the fall of Jerusalem, which happened a few decades after His death, and the end of the world as we know it when Jesus will return as Judge of all the earth. Bible scholars disagree on the interpretation of Matthew 24. Some see it entirely about the destruction of Jerusalem, while others say parts of it relate to the destruction of Jerusalem and parts to the end of the world. A third view is that the destruction of Jerusalem foreshadows the events leading up to the end of the world. While it might lead to intriguing discussions, we're not going to resolve this question in our study today. Instead, we're going to get a feel for the apocalyptic language.

What was the disciples' natural response to Jesus's prediction in verse 2?

What signs did Jesus list for them (vv. 4-7)?

Today, we seldom hear people claiming to be the Christ, but it's striking that Jesus's first response to His disciples' interest in the signs surrounding His return was to warn them against false teachers. There are certainly plenty of false teachers today who are claiming to have insight into the end times! Then, Jesus listed events, man-made and natural, that have taken place throughout history—wars, earthquakes, famines.

What metaphor did He use to describe these kinds of things in verse 8?

Jesus used related language in Matthew 19, when He pointed forward to "the renewal of all things, when the Son of Man sits on his glorious throne" (Matt. 19:28). The word translated as "renewal" can mean "regeneration" or "rebirth."[4] Each of us needs to be born again to see God's kingdom. But in the end, the world itself will also be born again!

In Matthew 24:9-13, what did Jesus say would happen to His true followers and those who only profess to follow Him?

What did Jesus say will happen before the end in verse 14?

What situation foreseen by the prophet Daniel did Jesus reference in verse 15?

READ DANIEL 9:27; 11:31; 12:11.

In Matthew 24:15, Jesus said "let the reader understand," but it's not as simple as an ancient IYKYK (if you know, you know). Again, there is a sense in which this prophecy was fulfilled at the destruction of the temple in AD 70. The Romans leveled the building and made sacrifices to their pagan gods. But this may have been only a partial fulfillment of Jesus's prophecy, which will be fully fulfilled in the run-up to the final judgment day.

In verses 16-21, Jesus gave advice and warnings about the seriousness of the coming disaster.

What did He warn His disciples about once again in verses 23-26? Why do you think He continued to return to this theme throughout His teaching?

Jesus did not want His followers to be misled. He told them that when He did actually come, there was no way anyone would miss it (v. 27).

In verse 28, Jesus made a seemingly straightforward observation from nature. Clearly, we're meant to draw an analogy of some sort between carrion birds gathering to a corpse and the events Jesus describes, but scholars have debated multiple possible options, and there is no clear consensus. As Jesus continued His discourse, the apocalyptic language built.

READ MATTHEW 24:29-35. What did Jesus say will happen right after the distress of those days in verse 29? What does that language seem to indicate?

Taken literally, Jesus's description sounds like the end of the universe. But this kind of language was used in the Old Testament to describe God's mighty acts of judgment and deliverance (see Jer. 4:23-28; Ezek. 32:6-8), as well as to describe the day of the LORD (see Isa. 13:9-10; 24:21-23; Joel 2:1-10). So, again, there is some debate as to whether Jesus was referring to the final judgment day or the destruction of Jerusalem.

How did Jesus describe His entrance in Matthew 24:30-31?

Jesus's language here clearly echoes Daniel's vision of "one like a son of man" coming on the clouds in Daniel 7. Taken at face value, it sounds very much like the final judgment. But in verse 34, Jesus declared, "Truly I tell you, this generation will certainly not pass away until all these things take place." So, if we take "this generation" literally, it suggests that "all these things" took place, at least in some sense, at the destruction of Jerusalem in AD 70, even if those events are also foreshadowing the future day of judgment. As with many

Old Testament prophecies, we likely need to recognize a short-term, partial fulfillment while also keeping a long-term final fulfillment in our line of sight. And verse 36 can serve as a warning against thinking we know more than we do: "Now concerning that day and hour no one knows—neither the angels of heaven nor the Son—except the Father alone."

In the rest of Matthew 24, Jesus continued to issue warnings about future judgment. Then, in Matthew 25, He told three parables about the judgment day, the last of which is His famous parable of the sheep and the goats (Matt. 25:31-46). This all leads up to Matthew's narrative about Jesus's betrayal and arrest. But Jesus spoke in apocalyptic terms again when He was on trial for His life in Matthew 26.

> **READ MATTHEW 26:62-68.** What apocalyptic reference did Jesus make, and how did the religious leaders react to this claim?

The high priest and the other members of the Sanhedrin clearly didn't believe that Jesus's apocalyptic prophecy that He is the One who will fulfill Daniel's vision was true. They saw it as blasphemy. But Matthew goes on to tell the story of Jesus's death and resurrection, and his Gospel ends with Jesus's earth-shattering claim that He really is the rightful King of all the earth:

> All authority has been given to me in heaven and on earth. Go, therefore, and make disciples of all nations, baptizing them in the name of the Father and of the Son and of the Holy Spirit, teaching them to observe everything I have commanded you. And remember, I am with you always, to the end of the age.

> *MATTHEW 28:18b-20*

Jesus's apocalyptic pronouncements in the Gospels give us a powerful impression of what will happen in the final days, but exactly when and how these prophecies will be fulfilled is not revealed. If there's one thing we know for sure about the Bible's apocalyptic prophecies, however, it's that Jesus Christ—the Lamb who was slain—stands at the center and will be revealed in all His terrifying glory when He comes again as Judge of all the earth. We must all be ready for that day.

DAY 5

PROPHECY

I generally like food. But there's a short list of commonly ingested items that I find deeply disgusting. Mustard is one of them. I could just tell you, "I hate mustard." But if I said instead, "I hold this truth to be self-evident, that mustard should never be put on a burger," you'd know I was channeling the Declaration of Independence to make my point. In any culture, there are certain texts—ancient and modern—that everyone is expected to know so that they can be quoted or alluded to and everyone will get it.

So far this week, we've looked at prophecy from multiple angles, ranging from straight-up prediction to apocalyptic. In our final day of study, we're going to look at some examples of direct and indirect quotations from Old Testament prophecies in the Gospels. Jews of Jesus's day would have known the Old Testament Scriptures very well—not from reading the text themselves but from hearing it read and taught. They would have picked up on allusions that you and I need help to recognize. Sometimes, the direct citation of an Old Testament text is like the tip of an iceberg. We need to see the rest of the text beneath the surface of the narrative to understand its meaning and importance. We'll look at one example from the beginning of Jesus's public ministry in Luke and an example from the end of it in Matthew.

In Luke 4, Jesus was preaching His first recorded sermon in His hometown synagogue. He stood up to read from the scroll of the prophet Isaiah and found Isaiah 61.

READ LUKE 4:16-21. What did the speaker claim about Himself in the Isaiah quotation?

LOOK BACK AT LUKE 3:21-22. What connection do you see between Jesus's baptism and His first public sermon in Luke?

What did the speaker in Isaiah claim he'd been anointed and sent to do?

What claim did Jesus make about Isaiah's prophecy in verse 21?

The spot in the text where Jesus stopped reading is significant. His audience would likely have known that in Isaiah 61:2, "to proclaim the year of the LORD's favor," is followed by "and the day of our God's vengeance." At that moment, Jesus was opening the window of opportunity for salvation. The day of God's vengeance against His enemies had not yet come.

Observant Jews of Jesus's day would have been far more familiar with Old Testament texts than most of us are today. Rather than each having their own Bibles to refer to, they would have been much more dependent on memorization. Often when the Gospel authors drew connections between Jesus's life and the Hebrew Scriptures, they expected their readers to be familiar with a passage beyond the portion that was directly quoted.

Matthew is the Gospel author most known for citing Old Testament texts and showing their fulfillment in the life of Jesus, but he also embedded allusions to the Hebrew Scriptures in his narratives without always calling them out. In Matthew's account of Jesus's trial, abuse, and crucifixion, the explicit quotation from the Hebrew Scriptures comes from Jesus Himself when He quoted the beginning of Psalm 22 in Aramaic: "'*Elí, Elí, lemá sabachtháni?*' that is, 'My God, my God, why have you abandoned me?'" (Matt. 27:46). But Jewish readers of Matthew's Gospel would likely have spotted parallels with Psalm 22 throughout the crucifixion account.

READ PSALM 22:1-18 AND MATTHEW 27:27-50. Psalm 22 was written by King David: the archetypal king of the Jews. What were the Roman soldiers mocking Jesus for claiming to be in verses 27-31?

Note which verses in Matthew's account echo the following verses in Psalm 22 and how:

Verse 7

Verse 8

Verse 18

In John's account, the connection with Psalm 22:18 is made explicitly. When the soldiers crucified Jesus, they took His clothes and divided them into four parts, a part for each soldier. They also took the tunic, which was seamless, woven in one piece from the top.

> So they said to one another, "Let's not tear it, but cast lots for it, to see who gets it." This happened that the Scripture might be fulfilled that says: They divided my clothes among themselves, and they cast lots for my clothing. This is what the soldiers did.

JOHN 19:24

But while Jesus was evidently fulfilling Psalm 22 in His crucifixion, Psalm 22 does not explicitly predict the crucifixion as a future event. Rather, it foreshadows it, as God's anointed King (David) described his suffering in terms that God's ultimate anointed King (Jesus) would finally fulfill. Take some time to reflect on Jesus as the fulfillment of all the Old Testament Scriptures—both those that make direct predictions and those that foreshadow His identity and work.

How has your study this week helped you to see the rich and complex connections between the Hebrew Scriptures and Jesus as revealed in the Gospels?

How does Jesus's ability both to fulfill prophecy from the past and to speak prophetically about the future show His universal power over time and space?

How does the fulfillment of Old Testament prophecy in the Gospels help you understand more of the gospel message of Jesus as the Son of God, who suffered and died in our place for the forgiveness of our sins and will one day return to judge as the resurrected Lord of all?

UNDERSTANDING PROPHECY

IN THE GOSPELS >

Tips

We've seen this week that prophecy in the Gospels is not just about straightforward prediction, though it certainly can feature prediction. Here are the four different kinds of writing that can help us navigate prophecy in the Gospels:

Prediction: A description of what will happen in the future. We see this in the Gospels both as Old Testament prophecies are fulfilled and as Jesus makes predictions about what will happen in the future.

Poetry: A powerful form of communication that often features metaphors and parallelism (especially in the Bible), as ideas from one line are repeated in the next using different text.

Personification: When a group of people or a non-human entity is written about as if they were a human being (for example, when Wisdom is personified as a woman in the book of Proverbs, when God is described as having a strong arm, or when Israel is pictured as God's wife).

Apocalyptic: Writing that points to the end times and God's dramatic intervention, often expressed in metaphorical language.

Prophecy in the Gospels is often complex and multifaceted, and we should be careful not to try to reduce it down to simple prediction. Instead, we should recognize the range of (sometimes surprising) ways in which the Gospels connect Jesus's life, death, and resurrection to Old Testament texts, and we should have a humble approach as we read prophecy about future events in the Gospels, recognizing that we may not fully understand it until after it has been fulfilled.

Exercise

Listed below are three passages that feature different forms of prophecy in the Gospels. Read each passage and complete the prompts that follow to help you better recognize and understand how and when different types of prophecy are used.

READ MARK 1:1-11. How does Mark's opening show Old Testament prophecy being fulfilled?

How is this passage also an example of prophecy being made within the Gospels?

To what extent is John the Baptist's prophecy about Jesus fulfilled in this passage?

Where do you see poetry in this passage?

Where do you see parallelism?

READ MATTHEW 3:11-12. What kind of prophecy did John the Baptist use here?

Apocalyptic prophecy often includes vivid metaphors. What metaphor did John use here?

READ LUKE 13:31-35. Where do you see personification in this passage?

Where do you see prediction?

Jesus quoted Psalm 118:26, "Blessed is he who comes in the name of the Lord!" How does Jesus's triumphal entry into Jerusalem (see Luke 19:28-40) fulfill this Old Testament text and this New Testament prediction?

Wrap-up

This isn't the end. It's the beginning! Now that you've spent time examining the different genres in the Gospels and honing your skill in reading them, why not set a goal of reading through all the Gospels and identifying the different kinds of writing as you come to them?

The categories we've looked at in this study aren't rigid. You might come to a saying of Jesus and think, *Wait, is this a parable or just a slightly extended metaphor?* It's a good question to ask as it shows you're noticing the text, but scholars debate these boundaries, and in some instances, there isn't a "right answer." Like when you're skiing, there are sometimes two equally good ways to navigate a section of the slope.

We've traversed across all four Gospels in our study, but the Gospels are designed to be read straight through. Doing so will give you a wonderful view of Jesus. Mark's Gospel is a great place to start. It's the shortest Gospel and very likely the first to be written. So while it's not the first in order in our Bibles, many of the first readers of the other Gospels would have read Mark before they read Matthew, Luke, or John.

Once you've finished reading through the Gospels, you'll have a richer, deeper understanding of who Jesus is and what that means for you. But you will still have more to learn and enjoy because Jesus is always more than we could ask or imagine. One day we will get to see Jesus with our own eyes, but until then, we can meet Him in His Word. As the author of John's Gospel put it near the end of his biography, "Jesus performed many other signs in the presence of his disciples that are not written in this book. But these are written so that you may believe that Jesus is the Messiah, the Son of God, and that by believing you may have life in his name" (John 20:30-31).

My prayer for you, and for myself, as we go deeper with the Gospels is that we would be more and more convinced that Jesus is the everlasting Son of God, who came to live and die and rise again for us so we could live eternally with Him. Let's savor that relationship today and set our sights on that great future day when Jesus will come back to rule the world, wipe every tear from our eyes, and wrap us in His arms forevermore. Amen. Come, Lord Jesus!

SESSION *Eight*

To access the video teaching sessions, use the instructions in the back of your Bible study book.

NOTES

Watch Rebecca's Session Eight video.

Download the *Navigating Gospel Truth* leader guide at **lifeway.com/gospeltruth**

GROUP DISCUSSION GUIDE

What was your favorite session of study? Why?

What is your main takeaway from this Bible study?

How will you apply what you've learned?

After doing this study, do you feel better equipped to understand and apply the Scripture? Explain.

If someone asked you, "Why should I do the study *Navigating Gospel Truth*?" what would you tell them?

WRAP-UP ❯

Here's a reading plan to follow if you want to read all four Gospels over the next eight weeks.

			READ THE GOSPELS IN EIGHT WEEKS			
	DAY 1	DAY 2	DAY 3	DAY 4	DAY 5	DAY 6
WEEK 1	Mark 1–2	Mark 3–4	Mark 5–6	Mark 7–8	Mark 9–10	Mark 11–12
WEEK 2	Mark 13–14	Mark 15–16	Matt. 1–2	Matt. 3–4	Matt. 5–6	Matt. 7–8
WEEK 3	Matt. 9–10	Matt. 11–12	Matt. 13–14	Matt. 15–16	Matt. 17–18	Matt. 19–20
WEEK 4	Matt. 21–22	Matt. 23–24	Matt. 25	Matt. 26	Matt. 27	Matt. 28
WEEK 5	Luke 1	Luke 2	Luke 3–4	Luke 5–6	Luke 7–8	Luke 9–10
WEEK 6	Luke 11–12	Luke 13–14	Luke 15–16	Luke 17–18	Luke 19–20	Luke 21–22
WEEK 7	Luke 23–24	John 1	John 2–3	John 4–5	John 6–7	John 8–9
WEEK 8	John 10–11	John 12–13	John 14–15	John 16–17	John 18–19	John 20–21

ENDNOTES

Session One

1. Richard Bauckham, *Jesus: A Very Short Introduction* (Oxford: Oxford University Press, 2011), 55–56.

2. For Richard Bauckham's argument, see *Jesus and the Eyewitnesses* (Grand Rapids, MI: Eerdmans Publishing Company, 2006), 420–423, 458–468.

3. Bart D. Ehrman, *Truth and Fiction in The Da Vinci Code* (Oxford: Oxford University Press, 2004), 102.

4. Bauckham, *Jesus and the Eyewitnesses,* 102.

5. Bauckham, *Jesus and the Eyewitnesses,* 71–72.

6. Bauckham, *Jesus and the Eyewitnesses,* 89.

7. Peter J. Williams, Twitter post, Oct. 23, 3018, https://twitter.com/drpjwilliams/status/1054751290901909504?lang=en.

8. Mounce quotes Ehrman noting that his doctoral supervisor believed that "the essential Christian beliefs are not affected by textual variants in the manuscript tradition of the New Testament," and adds, "For the most part, I think that's true." See William D. Mounce, *Why I Trust the Bible* (Grand Rapids: Zondervan, 2021), 141; Bart D. Ehrman, *Misquoting Jesus: The Story Behind Who Changed the Bible and Why* (San Francisco: HarperOne, 2005), 252.

Session Two

1. Flavius Josephus, *The Works of Josephus, with a Life Written by Himself,* trans. from the original Greek (New York: Oakley, Mason and Co. 1879), 303.

2. Richard Bauckham, *Gospel Women* (Grand Rapids, MI: William B. Eerdmans Publishing Company, 2002), 290–292.

3. Strong's G2334, Blue Letter Bible, https://www.blueletterbible.org/lexicon/g2334/csb/mgnt/0-1/.

4. Bart D. Ehrman, *Jesus, Interrupted* (New York: HarperOne, 2009), 48.

5. Strong's G32, Blue Letter Bible, https://www.blueletterbible.org/lexicon/g32/kjv/tr/0-1/.

6. Celsus, as quoted by Richard Bauckham, *Gospel Women,* 271.

Session Three

1. Strong's H5288, Blue Letter Bible, https://www.blueletterbible.org/lexicon/h5288/kjv/wlc/0-1/.

2. Strong's H7716, Blue Letter Bible, https://www.blueletterbible.org/lexicon/h7716/kjv/wlc/0-1/.

3. *Harry Potter and the Half-Blood Prince,* directed by David Yates (Warner Bros. Pictures, 2009).

4. Gerald L. Borchert, *John 1–11,* vol. 25A, The New American Commentary (Nashville: Broadman & Holman Publishers, 1996), 165.

Session Four

1. Klyne Snodgrass, *Stories with Intent: A Comprehensive Guide to the Parables of Jesus, 2nd ed.* (Grand Rapids, MI: Eerdmans Publishing Company, 2018), 45.

Session Five

1. *Talmud* (Shabbat 31a), quoted in Shoshannah Brombacher, "On One Foot," https://www.chabad.org/library/article_cdo/aid/689306/jewish/On-One-Foot.htm.

2. *The Sound of Music,* directed by Robert Wise (20th Century Fox, 1965).

3. George Thomas Kurian, *Nelson's New Christian Dictionary: The Authoritative Resource on the Christian World* (Nashville, TN: Thomas Nelson Publishers, 2001).

4. Gil Junger, *10 Things I Hate About You* (Buena Vista Pictures, 1999).

5. Peter J. Williams, *Can We Trust the Gospels?* (Wheaton, IL: 2018), 123–127.

6. Bauckham, *Jesus: A Very Short Introduction,* 60.

7. Bauckham, *Jesus: A Very Short Introduction,* 61.

Session Six

1. Gerald L. Borchert, *John 1–11,* 169.

2. Strong's G509, Blue Letter Bible, https://www.blueletterbible.org/lexicon/g509/kjv/tr/0-1/.

3. Borchert, *John 1–11,* 174.

4. Strong's G4151, Blue Letter Bible, https://www.blueletterbible.org/lexicon/g4151/kjv/tr/0-1/.

5. Strong's H7307, Blue Letter Bible, https://www.blueletterbible.org/lexicon/h7307/kjv/wlc/0-1/.

6. Borchert, 176–177.

7. Robert H. Mounce, *John,* The Expositor's Bible Commentary, Trembler Longman III and David E. Garland, eds. (Grand Rapids, MI: Zondervan, 2007).

8. Mark L. Strauss, *Exegetical Commentary on the New Testament* (Grand Rapids, MI: 2014), 311.

9. Strauss, 311.

10. Leon Morris, *The Gospel According to Matthew,* The Pillar New Testament Commentary (Grand Rapids, MI; Leicester, England: Eerdmans Publishing Company; Inter-Varsity Press, 1992), 404.

Session Seven

1. W. B. Yeats, "Aedh Wishes for the Cloth, 1899, https://poets.org/poem/aedh-wishes-cloths-heaven.

2. *Merriam-Webster,* s.v. "apocalypse," https://www.merriam-webster.com/dictionary/apocalypse.

3. Bruce B. Barton, *Matthew,* Life Application Bible Commentary (Wheaton, IL: Tyndale House Publishers, 1996), 474.

4. Strong's G3824, Blue Letter Bible, https://www.blueletterbible.org/lexicon/g3824/csb/mgnt/0-1/.

Get the most from your study.

IN THIS STUDY, YOU'LL:

- Affirm that the accounts of Jesus's life in the Gospels are reliable
  and true.

- Gain a clearer and more captivating view of Jesus's ministry
  and purpose.

- Cultivate an ability to read, understand, and interpret the different
  types of genres in the Bible.

To enrich your study experience, consider the accompanying *Navigating Gospel Truth* video teaching sessions, approximately 20–25 minutes, from Rebecca McLaughlin.

STUDYING ON YOUR OWN?

Watch Rebecca McLaughlin's teaching sessions, available via redemption code for individual video-streaming access, printed in this Bible study book.

LEADING A GROUP?

Each group member will need a *Navigating Gospel Truth* Bible Study Book, which includes video access. Because all participants will have access to the video content, you can choose to watch the videos outside of your group meeting if desired. Or, if you're watching together and someone misses a group meeting, she'll have the flexibility to catch up! A DVD set is also available to purchase separately if desired. You can access the free leader guide at lifeway.com/gospeltruth.

HERE'S YOUR VIDEO ACCESS.

To stream the *Navigating Gospel Truth* Bible study video teaching sessions, follow these steps:

1. Go to my.lifeway.com/redeem and register or log in to your Lifeway account.

2. Enter this redemption code to gain access to your individual-use video license:

IP23ZC4L3E

Once you've entered your personal redemption code, you can stream the video teaching sessions any time from your Digital Media page on my.lifeway.com or watch them via the Lifeway On Demand app on any TV or mobile device via your Lifeway account.

There's no need to enter your code more than once! To watch your streaming videos, just log in to your Lifeway account at my.lifeway.com or watch using the Lifeway On Demand app.

QUESTIONS? WE HAVE ANSWERS!
Visit support.lifeway.com and search "Video Redemption Code" or call our Tech Support Team at 866.627.8553.